Spitting at Dragons

Spitting at Dragons

Towards a
Feminist Theology of Sainthood

ELIZABETH STUART

MOWBRAY

Mowbray
A Cassell imprint
Wellington House, 125 Strand, London WC2R 0BB
127 W 24th Street, 4th Floor, New York, NY 10011

First published 1996

British Library Cataloguing-in-Publication Data
A catalogue record for this book is available from the British Library.

ISBN 0–264–67344–1

Typeset by Keystroke, Jacaranda Lodge, Wolverhampton.
Printed and bound in Great Britain by Redwood Books, Trowbridge, Wiltshire

Contents

For Penny Cassell

Preface

'When, when, O God, will the earth be ready for your saints?' cries
St Joan in Shaw's play about her life. This book aims to explore if
feminist theology is or ever will be ready for a theology of sainthood.
By feminist theology I mean that branch of theology which attempts
to reflect upon Christianity from the perspective of women. Certainly
feminist scholars have shown interest in women saints, but this
interest has generally focused upon attempting to offer feminist
readings of their lives. The whole concept of sainthood has been largely
ignored, consciously or unconsciously dismissed as beyond redemption, smacking as it does of spiritual élitism and other-worldly concerns
with which theologies of liberation have little concern. Many would
echo the sentiments of Monica Furlong in her declaration that
'unhappy is the Church that needs a saint' for such a Church is not
rooted in the ordinary and historical but in the extraordinary and
supernatural and has therefore lost the vision of its founder.[1] These
are concerns expressed and felt not only within Christian feminism
but within all theologies of liberation and, as these theologies exercise
an influence upon mainstream Christianity, at the centre as well as
the margins of the Church. I was brought up in the Roman Catholic
tradition and saints were an integral part of my early years. But I found
the way in which female saints were represented to be so off-putting
that when I was asked to choose a new name for my confirmation
I chose the name Augustine, much to the bewilderment of all concerned. Whilst my friends were opting for Bernadette, Theresa
and Mary, I wanted to identify with a saint who was assertive,
active, influential and a theologian (and I was quite conscious of this
at the age of eleven) but no female saint had ever been presented to
me in such terms and so I was forced to look to a man. The choice of
Augustine of Hippo is one I have been trying to live down ever since.
I am sure that my impression of the female saints as passive, suffering

embodiments of stereotypical femininity was shared by most Catholics of my generation and many generations before me.

But it has been a part of the Christian feminist project from the beginning to attempt to redeem at least the central beliefs of the Christian tradition from their patriarchal formulation. I began to see in the theology of sainthood as professed by the Roman Catholic and Orthodox Churches elements that hinted very strongly that redemption might be possible: the theology of sainthood is grounded in a concept of community; it is clearly a belief system that arose from the 'bottom up' and was often perceived by both the hierarchy and the laity as subversive, providing another system of authority beyond and above the clerical caste, and it was a process in which women were involved from the beginning – as saints, proclaimers of saints, and devotees of saints. So I began this exploration into the theology of sainthood from a feminist perspective. Readers curious for an explanation of the title are directed to the conclusion, where the story of St Elizabeth the Miracle-Worker is told.

I write as a white, European, Christian feminist rooted in the Roman Catholic tradition, whose primary objective is to wrestle with the religious tradition which formed me. Obviously my agenda(s) influence my theology and I unapologetically acknowledge them. I hope that other women from different contexts might add their perspectives so that Christian feminism develops a collection of theologies of sainthood. This book is but a small beginning, a preliminary exploration.

When I first began to study this topic I did not expect it to have much connection with my previous work, except in a general Christian feminist way, but I have found myself developing the theology of friendship that I attempted to expound in my writings on sexuality. This was prompted by the discovery that there is a clear tradition of speaking about saints in terms of friendship within Christianity. Again this simply reinforced my hunch that Christian feminists might find something in the concept of sainthood with which to work.

A number of books written in the 1980s on the subject of saints and sainthood came to the conclusion that the hierarchy of the Church no longer provides us with the saints we need. This is a clear invitation to those of us who do not exercise privileged positions of power within the ecclesial institution to reclaim both the theology and practice of canonization. I think that to a large extent women have reclaimed the latter; it is now time to reflect theologically on that practice.

I am grateful to Steve Cook for first suggesting I delve into this topic and to Judith Longman and Ruth McCurry for encouraging and enabling me to take it forward. The staff at the Bodleian Library, Catholic Central Library and the Learning Resources Centre at the University of Glamorgan were helpful and efficient in providing material. My thanks also to Elizabeth Herrington for her skills as an unofficial research assistant and to Jane Robson for reading and commenting on the text.

Elizabeth Stuart
The Feast of St Crispina, mother, martyr and friend to
Sts Maxima, Donatilla and Secunda

NOTE

1 Monica Furlong, 'Holiness in the continuing tradition' in Marina Chavchavadze (ed.), *Man's Concern with Holiness* (London: Hodder and Stoughton, 1970), p. 25.

Introduction

Saints are enjoying something of a popular and not so popular revival. Pope John Paul II has beatified and canonized more people than all his twentieth-century predecessors put together.[1] As of the end of October 1995 he had canonized 272 people and beatified 731.[2] The shelves dedicated to religion in general book shops groan with an increasing number of general books on the saints, usually in the form of dictionaries or annotated calendars. In 1995 the Church of England announced plans to enlarge its liturgical calendar to add to it more people who have not been proclaimed saints by the Roman Catholic or Orthodox Churches but who represent what the Bishop of Chichester described as 'a comfortable, moderate standard of holiness'.[3] The list, which is thoroughly ecumenical, included Florence Nightingale, C. S. Lewis, Samuel Johnson, Cardinal Newman, Pope John XXIII, Oscar Romero, William and Catherine Booth and George Fox, and was much discussed in the secular press. According to recent reports in the church press the practice of pilgrimage usually associated with specific saints is also experiencing something of a regeneration. Since the Second Vatican Council devotion to the saints may have become less fervent among North European and North American Catholics but if proof were needed that the concept of sainthood was still alive and well even in these parts of the world, it was provided in 1994. In that year the British television station Channel Four broadcast a programme made by the Bandung production company entitled *Hell's Angel: Mother Teresa of Calcutta*. This programme set out to draw attention to the popular canonization of this woman during her own lifetime and to ask some serious questions about some of her methods of caring for the dying destitute of Calcutta. The presenter Christopher Hitchens pointed out that 'the saintliness of an Albanian nun named Agnes Boyaxhiu is a proposition that is accepted by many who are not even believers'.[4]

[1]

A priest greeting her arrival at the shrine of Knock in the Republic of Ireland declared that 'no woman has made such an impact here since Our Lady herself appeared in 1879'.[5] Malcolm Muggeridge was credited with establishing Mother Teresa's saintly status in the West. Not only did he make an early documentary about her work in Calcutta but he was apparently convinced a miracle had taken place in the filming of it. A camera operator on the documentary related that it was so dark in the 'house of the dying' that the director was pessimistic about being able to film anything. But the crew had in their possession a new type of film which they had not yet tested and so decided to try it out. When viewing the rushes back in Britain they were amazed at the quality of the film.

> And I said that's amazing. That's extraordinary. And I was going to go on to say you know, three cheers for Kodak. I didn't get a chance to say that though because Malcolm sitting in the front row spun round and said 'It's divine light. It's Mother Teresa. You'll find that it's divine light old boy.' And three or four days later I found I was being phoned by journalists from London newspapers who were saying things like 'we hear you've just come back from India with Malcolm Muggeridge and you were the witness of a miracle.'[6]

The programme went on raise a number of questions about the saintliness of Mother Teresa. Grim pictures were painted of her hospice for the dying. Bad medical practice was hinted at and it was implied that people who could be saved were being left to die. But the bulk of the programme focused on Mother Teresa's campaign against abortion and contraception and her association with right-wing politicians. She was depicted as a 'roving ambassador of a highly politicised papacy',[7] accepting money and support from some of the most corrupt political regimes and individuals in the world whilst claiming to be non-political. The makers of the programme evidently felt that there was something deeply disturbing, incongruous and dangerous about 'a virgin who also campaigns against birth control' leading such a fierce battle against abortion, and someone who has devoted their lives to the poor but who believes, as Mihir Bose put it,

> that there's nothing much you can do for the poor except take them off the streets and, you know, look after them. You cannot change their attitudes, you cannot make them feel they have an ability, they may even have the means to improve and change their lives. She's not bothered with that agenda. She's only bothered with the agenda of trying to rescue their souls and making them a bit better before they go on to eternal life.[8]

Bose also suggested that part of the appeal of Mother Teresa to the West lay in the fact that a Western woman had sacrificed her life for the Third World. This example, of 'one of our own' heroically setting out to 'rescue' people less fortunate than ourselves, serves to salve our own consciences. Half a century ago Albert Schweitzer served the same purpose and his saintliness was also subsequently 'debunked'.

The programme maintained that, in return for her loyalty, Pope John Paul II was known 'to have placed her on the fast track for canonisation'.[9] But the makers evidently found it impossible to view this woman in the same light as the pontiff. The programme concluded:

> In a godless and cynical age it may be inevitable that people will seek to praise the self effacing, the altruistic and the pure in heart. But only a complete collapse of our critical faculties can explain the illusion that such a person is manifested in the shape of a demagogue, an obscurantist and a servant of earthly power.[10]

I will return to the figure of Mother Teresa later on in this book, but for the moment I simply want to draw attention to the extraordinary outcry that greeted this programme. Some people who had taken part in it attempted to distance themselves from it; Catholics and non-Catholics alike joined voices in howls of protest. It was frequently asserted by outraged viewers that, because Mother Teresa could not answer back, Channel Four was guilty of bias and unfairness, although it was never made clear why Mother Teresa could not answer back if she wished. But it was obvious that many felt that the programme had done something unpardonable in questioning the credentials of a 'living saint'. Anything that the Pope might do to her after her death would only be a formality, confirming a canonization by popular acclaim that happened many years ago. Dead saints may have lost some of their appeal but living ones are still venerated. It is also clear that even in a supposedly secularized world the concept of sainthood is still closely linked to religious belief and practice. When the pop star Bob Geldof launched the 'Band/Live Aid' project in the 1980s, the popular media took to referring to him as 'Saint Bob', but the label did not really fit or stick, partly perhaps because Geldof vigorously resisted it, partly because his life-style did not measure up to popular notions of holiness, but chiefly I think because his extraordinary vision and determination was not motivated by any overt orthodox religious beliefs.

In the academic world, too, saints have been brought in from the cold. Since the Enlightenment, with its concern for historical 'truth', hagiography has been regarded with suspicion. Historians, in particular the group of Jesuit scholars known as the Bollandists, have concerned themselves with attempting to sift fact from fiction in the lives of the saints.[11] Other than historians, it is specialists in folk lore who have shown most interest in the lives of the saints. However, since 1980, sociologists, philosophers and theologians have turned their attention to the saints. Lawrence Cunningham attributes renewed interest amongst theologians to a number of theological trends: 'The emergence of the study of spirituality as a discrete discipline, the serious interest in narratology, and the turn towards the analysis of religious experience have provoked a renewed concern with the saintly life as a locus for theological reflection.'[12] As Cunningham mentions, the development of narrative theology encouraged some late twentieth-century theologians to take a serious interest in the lives of the saints. Particularly associated with Stanley Hauerwas, George Lindbeck and Hans Frei, narrative theology has sought to shift the emphasis off abstract and propositional theology and ethics and on to story, believing that human beings are fundamentally story-telling beings who think in terms of narrative and receive moral guidance from stories rather than abstract morals. Most narrative theologians maintain that it is the grand story of the Bible that enables us to make sense of the stories of our own lives. In 1974 James William McClendon Jr published a pioneering work on what would be later labelled narrative theology in which he attempted to place the lives of the saints at the heart of such a theology.

> By recognizing that Christian beliefs are not so many 'propositions' to be catalogued or juggled like truth-functions in a computer, but are living convictions which give shape to actual lives and actual convictions which give shape to actual lives and communities, we open ourselves to the possibility that the only relevant critical examination of Christian beliefs may be one which begins by attending to lived lives. Theology must be at least biography. If by attending to those lives, we find ways of reforming our own theologies, making them more true, more faithful to our ancient vision, more adequate to the age now being born, then we will be justified in that arduous inquiry. Biography at its best will be theology.[13]

In the lives of the saints we are presented with biography as theology. In every age Christian communities have venerated men and women whose stories reflect the great story of the life of Christ to an extraordinary degree and whose lives challenge our own and our understanding of the great life. McClendon chose to focus on several non-canonized individuals of the twentieth century, including Martin Luther King and Dag Hammarskjöld, drawing particular attention to the understanding of the doctrine of the atonement that could be read off these two lives. However, narrative theology has failed to live up to its early promise to provide new theological insights from the lives of the saints.

An interesting approach to the lives of the saints was taken by philosopher Edith Wyschogrod, who attempted to relate them to post-modern philosophy. In particular she believed that the saints could help provide an alternative to modern ethical systems which had produced immoral behaviour. Wyschogrod isolated four areas in which the lives of the saints and the concerns of post-modern philosophy coincide: the saints' lives are communicated in and as texts; the narrative of the saint's life is in itself a locus for reflection and action; the lives are often concerned with the body and the need to control and transform it; the lives of the saints are grounded in reality and hence they 'read the reader', challenging her.[14] David Matthew Matzko has developed Wyschogrod's ideas further, arguing that post-modernism is not a time in which new ideas of sainthood can emerge but it is a time in which 'saints who emerge from local traditions and communities can have a renewed force in creating human community'.[15] Saints are profoundly subversive of modern thought concepts, they are in fact 'scandals' in the modern world, for they undermine the modernist idols of rationality, universality and democracy.

Sociologists have used the lives of the saints as tools for understanding both popular religion and the societies in which the saints lived and in which their lives were written.[16]

Narrative theology may have never quite followed through its initial interest in the saints but other theologies have stepped into the breach. Liberation theology, in seeking to do theology from the basis of the experience of the poor, marginalized and invisible in Latin America, has had to take devotion to the saints seriously. In the lives of the saints the people find a 'subversive memory', a continuance of that found in the scripture stories of the Exodus, which empower them to struggle against injustice meted out against them often in the name of Christ.[17] Eduardo Hoornaert in his study of Christian history from the perspective of the poor of Latin America has argued that the history of the early Church is the history of communities, not hierarchies. Some of their history has been lost, consigned to oblivion by the powerful, and needs to be re-membered, some is preserved in the stories of the saints of the early Church. Feminism has shown a consistent interest in female hagiography. Perhaps the earliest and most widespread attitude to the stories of female saints is represented by Mary Daly:

> Surviving, moving women can hardly look to the masochistic martyrs of sadospi. ʼal religion as models. Since most patriarchal writing that purports to deal with women is pornography or hagiography (which amount to the same thing), women in a world from which women-identified writing has been eliminated are trying to break away from these mouldy 'models', both of writing and of living.[18]

She prefers to write Hag-ography, the story of the Great Hags of women's hidden history, those whom 'the institutionally powerful but privately impotent patriarchs found too threatening for coexistence, and whom historians erase'.[19] The lives of the women saints were almost invariably (but not exclusively) written by men who sought to conform those lives to contemporary notions of what constituted 'holiness'. This usually involved for women some kind of escape from their frail and sinful womanly nature and embodiment and self-abasement and obedience to male representatives of the Church. What possible use could such life stories be in the feminist project except as specific examples of patriarchal brutality?

Yet many feminists believe the situation is actually more complex than that. For a start, in the lives of the saints women are made visible in a patriarchal context. They are not written out of history altogether. Their lives, however much her-story has been overwritten by his-story, at least provide Christian women with a collection of ancestors in faith, a tradition of active, appreciated and powerful women in which to ground our struggle for justice and from which to draw inspiration and strength. Lawrence Cunningham has made the point that in many respects the stories of the saints are unlike church history as a whole:

> There are more women represented; the *Untermenschen* have their moment; there is room for the neurotic, the naive, the unlovely as well as for the forceful and attractive personality. If I may borrow from contemporary Christology: Hagiography is Christianity from below rather than from above.... Since hagiography is the story of Catholicism told 'from below', it has been less susceptible to the restrictions of official scrutiny. That freedom brought with it a certain extravagance, that, at times, became excessive ... but it also revealed

a side of Christianity often overlooked in the official sources of Church history. The story of women in the Church is a case in point.[20]

Because hagiography emerges from the bottom up it is possible to trace the development of traditions and map the rewriting of women's lives, a practice that often reveals a woman very unlike the 'masochistic martyr' described by Daly. Because sainted women were often the subject of adulation in their lifetime, their writings sometimes survive, providing us with valuable insight into the position of women in the Church and the self-understanding and theological reflection of women of different times and circumstances. Many feminist scholars have used the lives of women saints in the project to retrieve and rescue the female voice in Christianity – the work of Elisabeth Schüssler Fiorenza, Rosemary Radford Ruether and Eleanor McLaughlin is particularly well known.[21] Feminist theologians and feminists of other disciplines have re-read the lives of the saints from a feminist perspective, some arguing that what on the surface may seem simply to present a patriarchal model of the feminine may actually, when read with the eyes of a woman-identified woman, reveal something altogether different – strength, originality, defiance and resistance.[22]

The recovery of the lost voices of women from church history is a vital enterprise for us women who choose to stand our ground within Christianity. We need a memory to sustain, strengthen and challenge us. Yet whilst feminist theology has paid close attention to the lives of women saints, it has not paid much attention at all to the theology of sainthood. For the past twenty years feminist, womanist and *mujerista*[23] theologians have gone about the task of revealing the androcentric (and white and Western) bias of Christian theology. As well as deconstructing the androcentric models of Christian theology, they have sought to reconstruct key aspects of Christian theology from the perspective of self-identified, self-affirming women. Models of God, christology, ecclesiology, the theology of marriage, ethics and Mariology have all been subjected to intense analysis and feminist reconstruction, but not the theology of sainthood. There are reasons for this which will be gone into later. However, it seems to me that the study of female saints naturally leads on to a consideration of the theology of sainthood. The increased interest in saints both inside and outside of academic circles would make such a study appropriate and opportune, as would the sheer increase in the number of saints in the past twenty years and the obvious and unapologetically

Spitting at dragons

political nature of the canonization process as it is carried out in the Roman Catholic Church. To give but one example at this stage. In September 1995 the Vatican newspaper *L'Osservatore Romano* carried an article from Mgr Helmut Moll, a Vatican official. Mgr Moll reported that the Church was actively looking for married couples to canonize.

> In this period when marriage and the family are under the strain of heavy burdens, there is a need for convincing examples . . . Staying together in good times and bad, in sickness and in health shows a heroic degree of virtue . . . We mean people whose love has never faded, whose promise of mutual fidelity has never been broken, and who unmasked such false solutions as 'trial marriage' or 'limited marriage'.[24]

The Vatican wants saints who will project its own theology of marriage, a theology which many women believe has a profoundly androcentric bias.[25] There can be no doubt that the theology of sainthood and the politics of canonization have been deployed against self-affirming women for centuries, but then so has christology and ecclesiology and Mariology – all the more reason for feminist theologians to reclaim the doctrine and perhaps also the process, particularly since women have always been part of them in a much more explicit and possibly more powerful way than in any other aspect of Christian theology. Is it possible that Daly is wrong and that Hag-ography can be done with feminist integrity within the Christian tradition? Daly would, of course, brook no possibility of this. For she is convinced that Christianity is inherently and irredeemably patriarchal. But for those of us who take what I believe to be the ultimate act of faith for a feminist woman and choose to believe that Christianity is transformable, re-makable, redeemable from patriarchy, and that the beliefs, practices and symbols that have oppressed us have also in some way provided us with the tools to overcome that oppression, no aspect of Christian belief can go unexamined by feminist theology. It is my intention in this book to explore the possibility of a feminist theology of sainthood.

NOTES

1 Kenneth L. Woodward, *Making Saints: Inside the Vatican: Who Become Saints, Who Do Not and Why* (London: Chatto and Windus, 1991), pp. 119–21.

2 *The Tablet* (28 October 1995), p. 1390.

3 *Independent on Sunday* (16 July 1995), p. 25.

4 Bandung Limited, *Hell's Angel: Mother Teresa of Calcutta* (transcript; London: Bandung Limited, 1994), p. 1.

5 Bandung Limited, *Hell's Angel*, p. 2.

6 Bandung Limited, *Hell's Angel*, p. 3.

7 Bandung Limited, *Hell's Angel*, p. 14.

8 Bandung Limited, *Hell's Angel*, pp. 11–12.

9 Bandung Limited, *Hell's Angel*, p. 14.

10 Bandung Limited, *Hell's Angel*, p. 16.

11 The Bollandists are named after John van Bolland (1596–1665) who began the task of producing critical accounts of the lives of the saints based upon 'authentic' material. These accounts are published in the *Acta Sanctorum*, which runs into over 50 volumes.

12 Lawrence S. Cunningham, 'A decade of research on the saints: 1980–1990', *Theological Studies*, vol. 53 (Summer 1992), p. 517.

13 James Wm McClendon Jr, *Biography As Theology: How Life Stories Can Remake Today's Theology* (New York: Abingdon Press, 1974), pp. 37–8.

14 Edith Wyschogrod, *Saints and Postmodernism: Revisioning Moral Philosophy* (Chicago: University of Chicago Press, 1990).

15 David Matthew Matzko, 'Postmodernism, saints and scoundrels', *Modern Theology*, vol. 9 (January 1993), p. 19.

16 See, for example, Stephen Wilson, *Saints and Their Cults: Studies in Religious Sociology, Folklore and History* (Cambridge: Cambridge University Press, 1983); and Donald Weinstein and Rudolph M. Bell, *Saints and Society: The Two Worlds of Western Christendom, 1000–1700* (Chicago: University of Chicago Press, 1982).

17 Eduardo Hoornaert, *The Memory of the Christian People* (Tunbridge Wells: Burns and Oates, 1988).

18 Mary Daly, *Gyn/Ecology: The Metaethics of Radical Feminism* (London: The Women's Press, 1979), p. 14.

19 Daly, *Gyn/Ecology*, p. 14.

20 Lawrence Cunningham, *The Meaning of Saints* (San Francisco: Harper and Row, 1980), p. 5.

21 See Elisabeth Schüssler Fiorenza, *In Memory of Her: A Feminist Theological Reconstruction of Christian Origins* (London: SCM, 1983); and Rosemary Radford Ruether and Eleanor McLaughlin, *Women of Spirit: Female Leadership in the Jewish and Christian Traditions* (New York: Simon and Schuster, 1979).

22 This has been the case particularly with St Thérèse of Lisieux. See, for example, J. W. Conn, 'Thérèse of Lisieux from a feminist perspective', *Spiritual Life*, vol. 28 (Winter 1982), p. 239. Other examples include Clarissa Atkinson, *Mystic and Pilgrim: The Book and World of Margery Kempe* (Ithaca: Cornell University Press, 1981).

23 Womanist theologians are African-American feminist theologians. The term *mujerista* refers to Spanish-speaking feminist women.
24 *The Tablet* (9 September 1995), p. 1152.
25 See my book *Just Good Friends: Towards a Lesbian and Gay Theology of Relationships* (London: Mowbray, 1995).

1

With friends like these: the problem

I have already touched upon the reasons as to why feminist theologians have shown little interest in the doctrine of sainthood, but it is important to spell these out in more detail.

No pain, no gain

Perhaps the most obvious reason is the way in which the women saints have been presented to us, in terms both of the texts of their lives and of the visual portraits painted or drawn. And that is to say nothing about the portraits of male saints and their attitude towards women. But I choose to concentrate upon female saints because it is to these that feminist theorists and theologians have turned their attention in the search for a female voice in Christian history and texts. Elisabeth Schüssler Fiorenza speaks for many Roman Catholic women when she describes her gradual disillusionment with the women saints who had populated her childhood:

> Maybe devotion to the Virgin and to the saints gave something to the male psyche, but we could not identify with the image of women presented by them. Our images of ourselves, our problems as young women, and our goals for life were totally different from the images of the female saints that were preached to us. The lives of the saints presented more of a hindrance than a help in finding our own self-identity. These stories stressed suffering, sexual purity, submission, outmoded piety, and total obedience. They were anti-intellectual and antierotic; they told about many nuns and widows and some queens, but rarely did they speak about ordinary women. While we desired our own independence and love, the glorification of the saints demanded humble feminine submission and fostered sexual neuroses.[1]

Let me illustrate the discomfort of feminist theorists initially with a couple of modern examples, lest anyone be tempted to think that the problem only lies in the 'unenlightened' past.

A *cause célèbre* for feminists is that of Maria Goretti (1890–1902) who became one of Italy's best loved saints. One of five children of a tenant farmer, Maria at the age of twelve fought off the advances of Alessandro Serenelli, the son of her father's partner. He intended to rape her but when she fought against him he stabbed her. He was reported to have threatened her with the knife, 'Submit or die', to which Maria replied 'Death but not sin!' Fatally wounded, Maria forgave her killer before passing away. The assailant was imprisoned for thirty years; he remained for eight years unrepentant until Maria appeared to him in a dream, gathering white lilies in a field and offering them to him. Alessandro then became a model prisoner and on his release went to Maria's mother to beg forgiveness. Maria quickly became a symbol of sexual purity and the patron of teenage girls and her beatification and canonization were rushed through at an unprecedented pace. Because she was regarded as a martyr a variety of miracles were not required of her, although many were reported, and in 1947 Pius XII beatified her, using the occasion to condemn unchastity in films, the fashion industry, theatre, youth in general and the military into which women had recently been conscripted in Italy. Three years later he declared her a saint in a ceremony that had to be held outside St Peter's because of the vastness of the crowd. In pious art Goretti is portrayed as looking rather older than her teenage years, with the looks of a 1940s film starlet: wrapped in a white cloak, her hands crossed over her chest, clutching lilies (symbols of purity). In 1985 an Italian journalist published a book in which he argued, on the basis of the records of Alessandro Serenelli's trial and the records of the canonization, that Alessandro may not have been guilty and that Maria may have 'given in'. He also argued that the Pope deliberately set out to make Maria a saint to counteract the sexual immorality that he believed Protestant American troops were bringing into Italy.[2] But for feminists the really disturbing nature of the story of Maria Goretti lies in its implicit messages. These are brought out by Ann Ball, in her uncritical account of the life of this saint, which begins: 'To many, the story of Maria Goretti is already familiar as the story of a young girl who refused to acquiesce in a grave sin against chastity.'[3] So even though her life was threatened, if Goretti had submitted to her assailant she would have 'acquiesced in a grave sin against chastity'. What message does this convey to victims of rape and abuse who have lived through their ordeal – that they are partly, at least, to blame? At the end of his account of Goretti's life Brother Kenneth CGA adds the following prayer:

'Lord, hold me back from sins of self-will, lest they get the better of me (Psalm 19.13).'[4] One might initially think that this prayer relates to Alessandro's behaviour, but every other prayer which follows an account of a saint's life in the book relates to the saint. Once again, then, the message is implicit, whether intentional or not, that Maria would have been guilty of sin if she had allowed the man to rape her. Rape is depicted in this life as a sin against sexual purity and therefore as primarily a sexual act, rather than an act of violence against the person as a whole. Through the telling of this story women are presented with only two choices when victims of male violence: 'submit' and share in the guilt or die. This is a theme that runs throughout female hagiography in one form or another.

When Goretti was canonized the Pope declared her 'the St Agatha of the twentieth century'. Veneration of Agatha can be traced back to the sixth century and according to her Acts she was a noble Christian who had dedicated her virginity to Christ. The Roman consul Quintianus used imperial edicts against Christianity to attempt to gain control over her. She was handed over to a woman (conveniently named Aphrodesia) who kept a brothel, but miraculously survived with her virginity. She was tortured and most famously of all her breasts were ripped off her, which is why she is usually depicted holding her breasts on a plate – pictures that led to some confusion among devotees who seem to have mistaken the objects for bread – which is blessed on her feast days – and possibly also for bells – hence her position as patron of campanology. Her breasts were restored though the miraculous intervention of St Peter. The authorities finally attempted to roast her naked on burning coals but the execution was interrupted by the eruption of Mount Etna and she either died in prison later, or was beheaded, or immediately gave up her spirit.

In another story told admiringly by Ann Ball, a young girl from Chile, Laura Vicuna (1891–1904), was subjected to advances from her widowed mother's lover which she managed to resist. Ball puts it like this: 'Through prayer and vigilance she determined to protect her purity. "Lord, do not let me offend You," she prayed.'[5] However, her main concern was for her mother, not because she was being abused by her lover but because she was 'living in sin' with him and had ceased to practise her Catholicism. When Laura was confirmed she 'begged her confessor to be allowed to offer her life to God for her mother's conversion. Realising that he was dealing with a person who had been given great spiritual gifts the priest granted her request.'[6]

And sure enough she became ill, necessitating her return from the convent school, where she boarded and was a model pupil, to the ranch. Her mother finally left her lover, an action which threw Señor Mora into a violent rage which he took out on Laura. She was beaten unconscious and survived for a week, during which she told her mother that she was offering her life for her. 'Mercedes [Laura's mother] fell to her knees sobbing. She realised what her daughter meant, and begged Laura's forgiveness as well as the forgiveness of God.'[7] After her daughter's death, Mercedes returned to the practice of her faith. The cause for Laura's canonization began in 1955. Here again we have a child bearing responsibility not only for threatened male violence but also for her mother's spiritual health. Once again the violence is masked beneath concerns for sins against impurity and the Catholic faith. The threat to Laura's mother for which her daughter offers her life comes not from the violence of her lover but from her 'sin' of living with him outside of marriage and her absence from the sacraments.

From its earliest days feminism has sought to unmask the violence that is often hidden within familial relationships and to name it for what it is – violence in which there is a perpetrator and a victim, and not simply one form of sexual behaviour in which both parties bear responsibility for what takes place. As Carol Adams has put it, 'If you hit someone over the head with a frying pan, you wouldn't call it cooking'.[8] Similarly, if someone threatens you with parts of the body commonly associated with the sexual act, do not call it sex; call it violence. Bound up with this masking of violence are notions about the difference between male and female sexuality which feminists have also sought to debunk, namely that men's sexual urges are a kind of 'tiger in the tank' stirring uncontrollably within them. Men can exercise some control of their tiger until it is awoken and prodded by women, who naturally ooze sexuality and therefore represent a real danger to men who wish to live 'pure' lives. They are, as one Orthodox hymnologist put it, 'snakier than the snake'.[9] Weinstein and Bell have pointed out that a comparison between the *vitae* (lives) of female and male saints of the Middle Ages reveals that when men are 'tempted' sexually the devil is usually blamed for interfering in the saint's life and has to be banished, but when women are subjected to the same kinds of temptation the temptation is envisaged as emanating not from a hostile outside force but from within them-selves: it is an essential part of women's nature to be 'lustful'.[10] This assumption about women's nature is evident in the stories of Goretti and Vicuna: they are both implicated by sexual interest in them, and only death clears them of blame. A British judge recently described the young female victim of a vicious rape as 'no angel' when explaining his inclination to be lenient towards her attacker. It is this mentality that lies behind the lives of thousands of women saints. They are portrayed as 'angels' because they would rather sacrifice their own life than live with the guilt and shame of being raped. St Rose of Lima, the first native of the New World to be declared a saint (she was canonized in 1671), was so frightened that she might be attractive to men that she scarred her face with pepper and her lips with quicklime and wore a crown of roses (with thorns) on her head. Once again we have a woman taking responsibility for how men may react to her.

It is deeply disturbing and unacceptable to feminists when this kind of reasoning is applied to any women, but it is particularly sickening when it is applied to children. Yet, as Thomas J. Heffernan has pointed out in his analysis of medieval hagiography, a female saint can only achieve sanctity if her virginity is constantly put at risk. 'It is only a beleaguered virginity that is able to gain the crown. The irony of the heroine's situation is that to gain sanctity through the maintenance of prized chastity, she must continually flaunt her virginity as a prize for her antagonists in her struggle toward saintly perfection.'[11] A vow of virginity in itself provokes desire and violence from men which women must resist again to the point of death – this is a constant theme in medieval hagiography and is embodied in the stories of such popular female saints as Katherine of Alexandria, Margaret of Antioch, Barbara and Juliana. The search for autonomy from men always provokes violence from men (usually fathers and/or suitors) and this must be resisted, to the point of death if necessary, in order to preserve virtue. Once again there are no heroic survivors in this situation: to survive in the end is to fail. Sara Maitland has noted that this was not always the case. Jesus, Peter and Paul all prayed to be delivered from martyrdom and the latter two both went to great lengths to avoid death. She attributes the growth of a collective masochistic drive for martyrdom to the growth of body/soul dualism in Christianity.[12]

Eamon Duffy in his study of the cult of women saints in fifteenth- and sixteenth-century England notes that Roman virgin martyrs were very popular during this period, being represented on rood screens. He comments that 'chastity was a virtue which featured very prominently in late medieval English religious sensibility' and this is reflected in the standard prayer-books for laity which implore the saints to protect the petitioner from lust and impurity.[13] An early thirteenth-century text, *Holy Maidenhood*, which sought to persuade young women to enter religious life, described the impurity of sex and marriage in lurid detail, calling upon the moral example of the 'blessed bond of gleaming maidens' Katherine of Alexandria, Margaret of Antioch, Agnes and Juliana. This emphasis can still be found at the heart of the Church's institutional power. In 1987, which was declared the 'Year of the Laity' in the Roman Catholic world, Pope John Paul II beatified three lay martyrs. None were married, two were women and both of these had resisted rape and died in the process.[14] Nor is the virgin's autonomy complete, for she rejects marriage to a human husband in order to become the bride of Christ; one form of marriage is exchanged for another. One form of submissiveness to men is exchanged for another which demands renunciation, pain and death. Complete autonomy for women is simply not an option. Sara Maitland offers a feminist analysis of the 'Bride of Christ' phenomenon. She notes that the devaluation of women within the Christian tradition goes hand in hand with an emphasis upon a relationship of passionate intimacy with the divine expressed in the language and imagery of heterosexuality. As long as the whole Christian community was regarded as the 'bride of Christ' the damage for women was limited, but once salvation became focused on the individual, 'the church, now rigidly personified as female, must be made manifest in every woman individually. Each woman, in a way that does not apply to men, must represent the Bride of Christ in her own person.'[15] This was made even more explicit in the life of a consecrated religious who had to go through an elaborate wedding ceremony with her divine spouse. Maitland argued that the rise of Romantic love in the late Middle Ages made matters worse because it was in essence the language of death.

> It inclines towards death, self-annihilation and suffering; it idolizes emotion above the object of the emotion; it rejects fulfilment and satisfaction necessarily . . . If it was bad enough to be the Bride of Christ, it is worse to be his romantic lover and still worse when the two become bound inextricably together, bride-and-lover in one. If romantic love was morbid for male lovers seeking earthly mistresses it is death itself for women seeking a heavenly master.[16]

Because women were associated with all that was evil and dangerous, they needed a good, strong man to knock them into shape and yet their perfect spouse Jesus was too good to punish them – indeed he suffered for them. This induced guilt which could only be soothed by self-inflicted punishment, and thus the erotic and the violent became intricately confused, as one twentieth-century religious noted:

> The purpose of flagellation was to dominate (to master) our sexuality. But sometimes when I hit myself I awakened my carnal desires. . . . By obedience to the Rule I had to use that device on myself every Monday, Wednesday and Friday. There was no escape. Many times masturbation happened . . . I felt guilty and remorseful and I requested heavy penance, which was granted. Heavy penance was self-inflicted flagellation, which sometimes aroused me again . . .[17]

Maitland argues that no penance is enough (except perhaps death) because you are repenting for what you are – a woman.

In the Roman Catholic Church there are three basic categories of saint: martyr, confessor and virgin, and several subcategories: pope, abbot, founder, apostle, evangelist, doctor of the Church and non-virgin. No men are to be found in the last subcategory despite the fact that someone like Augustine obviously fits the bill. He is described as a confessor, a doctor and a bishop in the liturgical calendar. But with the exceptions of Teresa of Avila and Catherine of Siena, the only women granted the status of Doctor of the Church (by Pope Paul VI in 1970), women have been bracketed either into the virgin/virgin-martyr or non-virgin categories.[18] This habit of classifying saintly women according to their sexual 'purity' does not of course endear the Church to feminists and may be thought to be symptomatic of the body-hating, anti-sexual ideology that has diseased Christianity for most of its history. The anti-body mentality is extolled in the lives of most female saints. Early and medieval and modern lives detail penances that women wrought on their own potentially evil bodies to subject them to the soul. Rose of Lima slept on bricks, used glass to pierce her flesh and filled her gloves with nettles. Flagellation, wearing shoes with nails piercing the feet, piercing the tongue and cheeks and sleeping on beds of thorns appear to have been *de rigueur* for the women saints of the late Middle Ages. As was excessive fasting. Sts Angela of Foligno and Elizabeth of Reute were reported to have gone without food (except for the Eucharist) for twelve and fifteen years respectively. It was noted in the Introduction that the Vatican has only just come round to the idea that married couples might make suitable candidates for canonization, so ingrained has been the association of sexuality and sin.

Those women who are classified under the 'non-virgin' category in the calendar include:

(a) Women who were widows who took vows of celibacy after their husbands' death, such as Sts Paula (famously associated with St Jerome), Melania the Elder, an early Church mother (i.e. ascetic), and Priscilla (who after the death of her husband is supposed to have allowed Peter to use her home as his Roman base).

(b) Women who married but then persuaded husbands to take a vow of celibacy. Included in this list are Hedwig of Bavaria who was married at the age of twelve in the thirteenth century to Henry, Duke of Silesia, but who did all she could to avoid having sex with him, never speaking to him in private and refusing to have sexual intercourse during Lent, on Sundays, holy days and when she thought she had conceived. Despite these measures she bore him six children. After 25 years of marriage she persuaded him to take a vow of chastity and she entered a convent. Also belonging to this category is Catherine of Sweden, daughter of St Brigid of Sweden. Catherine's mother had been forced into marriage by her father but found a husband equally reluctant to enjoy sexual relations. For two years Brigid and her husband did not consummate their marriage. In seeking divine guidance on how to deal with their desire for one another, they decided to have children and offer them to God, but this decision weighed heavily on their conscience – no doubt exasperated by baby Catherine's reported refusal to take her mother's breast when her mother had recently made love. Brigid forced Catherine against her will to marry at thirteen but Catherine persuaded her husband to respect her vow of virginity. Also famous in this regard was St Catherine of Conon, married at sixteen to an abusive husband, whose behaviour severely affected Catherine's health. Following a vision of Christ crucified she began to lead an ascetic life and eventually converted her husband. Both of them went to live in a small house and refrained from sexual relations.

(c) Some women attain sainthood through motherhood, i.e. through giving birth to people, usually men, who themselves become saints. A classic example of this is St Non, mother of Dewi Sant (St David) of Wales. Her story is told purely in terms of Dewi. According to one source she was a nun at Ty Gwyn in Dyfed and was raped by a prince. Once again in this ancient story the rape is masked by concerns for Non's modesty: 'In that meadow [where she was raped], too, at the time of her conception, two large stones . . . appeared, one at her head, and one at her feet; for the earth, rejoicing in the conceiving, opened its bosom, both in order to preserve the maid's modesty, and also to declare beforehand the significance of her offspring.'[19] Other sources report that she was the daughter of a Pembrokeshire chieftain and married to Sant (the rapist in the other story). Either way we hear nothing of her after her bringing to birth of Dewi.

We know more about St Monica, mother of Augustine, all of it from her saintly son. Monica's motherhood has been portrayed in two different ways: Augustine himself and pious devotees have presented her as 'the perfect mother' patiently praying and working for her husband's and son's conversion. Born into the Roman-Christian community at Carthage, Monica overcame an early drink problem when a servant took her to one side and, in her son's words, 'Bitterly she insulted her by bringing up the accusation that she was a boozer'.[20] Turning to sobriety and modesty, she was married to a pagan, Patrick, and tried to convert him to Christianity, despite his resolute unfaithfulness. Augustine proudly records that his father never hit his mother and, of course, this is because she knew how to handle him, never opposing him when he was angry. When other women complained about the violent abuse of their husbands,

> Monica, speaking as if in jest but offering serious advice, used to blame their tongues. She would say that since the day when they heard the so-called matrimonial contract read out to them, they should reckon them to be legally binding documents by which they had become servants. She thought they should remember their condition and not proudly withstand their masters. The wives were astounded, knowing what a violent husband she had to put up with.[21]

Just before his death Patrick became a Christian and then Monica turned her attention to her wayward son, sending away his mistress but keeping their son and at one point banning Augustine from her home until a priest advised against this behaviour. She then left him alone and simply prayed for his conversion which eventually occurred. She died soon after, claiming her life's work had been accomplished. Her heroic patience and persistence eventually secured her the patronage of married women and mothers. It was really in the Middle Ages that her cult began to take off. Her story is included in *The Golden Legend*, the thirteenth-century collection of the lives of the saints produced by Jacobus de Voragine, and it is possible to trace shifting understandings of motherhood through the way in which Monica is represented in art and narratives.[22] In the twentieth century Monica, like Mary and many other female saints, was drafted in by the Church in its fight against feminism. F. A. Forbes, writing her life in 1928, noted that Monica was great 'because she understood the sphere in which a woman's work in the world must usually be, and led her life truly along the lines that God had laid down for her'.[23] In recent times a more cynical reading of Monica's life has occurred and is caustically summed up by Sean Kelly and Rosemary Rogers, explaining how she managed to convert her husband and son:

> She ruthlessly employed a simple mother's method, tried and true, She wept. She sobbed. She snivelled. She bawled. Until in self-defence, Patrick was baptised and died, and Augustine abandoned his mistress to become a priest. In Southern California, the Spanish explorers found a rock spring that dripped and dribbled ceaselessly. They called it, and the town they founded nearby, Santa Monica.[24]

So the only way a sexually active woman achieves sainthood is through becoming the mother of a saint, and such instances are rare; otherwise virginity is the basic qualification. Even non-virgins turn out to be non-sexually active at least for a major part of their lives (this even applies to Monica). Maitland argues that, once outside 'pagan' forces could no longer be relied upon to martyr Christians, Christianity had become so masochistic that the only alternative was for the 'holy' to martyr themselves through virginity and other practices designed to conquer the flesh.

Related to this issue is the problem of ideals. Feminist theology has long maintained that Christian tradition has presented women with only two possibilities of being – virgin and mother. These are the ideals to which all women should aspire and in which alone they find wholeness, fulfilment and acceptability in the eyes of God. The perfect woman, the ultimate ideal, is of course Mary, both virgin and mother, an ideal unattainable for real women. Secular feminists have also drawn attention to the reduction of women to ideals in the media. These ideals, whether the Virgin Mother or the Page Three girl, are literally man-made. Women are expected to reduce themselves (often literally) to male notions of womanhood. Feminists may be reluctant to take the notion of sainthood seriously because it is undoubtedly true that the lives of women saints (and indeed their male counterparts) have often been reduced to ideals, moulded to fit into preconceived notions of sanctity.

Elissa R. Henken has produced two studies of the Welsh saints of the fifth and sixth centuries which reveal their lives to be highly patterned, modelled (most clearly in the case of male saints) on the folk heroes of their own land.[25] All the Welsh female saints have to flee from sexual advances and, with the exception of Ffraid, nothing is known of their lives before they begin to resist advances – it is this that defines and determines a saint's sanctity: the winning of her virginity, for example in the cases of Gwenfrewi, Melangell and Dwynwen, or (as in the case of Non) becoming a mother of a saint. This contrasts with the male saints whose sanctity is usually established at or before birth. Welsh women saints (unlike most of their male counterparts) usually flee their obstructive families and go to live in the woods or some other wild area. They tend to settle quietly in an area and, unlike their male counterparts, they do not found churches, gain rights of sanctuary or go on missionary journeys. Their miracles are largely domestic and usually associated with healing. Wells often spring up in their vicinity. Ffraid and Gwenfrewi both heal themselves as their first public miracle. Most drop from view before their deaths. Obviously this Welsh pattern is rather different from the Roman virgin-martyr pattern but it is still an ideal which conveys something of the society's attitude to women. There can be no doubt that the lives of many female saints have been moulded to fit patterns of sanctity established by a male-dominated Church. The individuality of the woman, her own personhood, is lost beneath 'ideals' and her life is then used to encourage other women to reduce their lives and possibilities to these narrow male ideals.

Various studies have shown how the lives of particular saints are changed and developed over time to fit changing ideals. Susan Haskins has mapped out the long and complex evolution of Mary Magdalen as 'myth and metaphor'.[26] Marina Warner has traced the changing profile of Joan of Arc from heretic and witch, through to nationalist heroine, guileless child of nature, and martyr.[27] Perhaps easier to grasp is Anne Thompson's study of the shaping of the life of St Frideswide of Oxford (*c.* 680–735), the founder of a double (male and female) monastery at Oxford, probably on the site of Christ Church. She was probably the daughter of a Mercian prince. Her first *vita* was written four centuries later by secular clerks living in her community. These clerks were expelled in the twelfth century when priestly celibacy was enforced. This, coupled with the fact that there

was a dispute between the priory and Abingdon Abbey over owner-
ship of the saint's body, led Robert Cricklade, head of St Frideswide's
Priory, to write a new *vita* (*c.* 1140) addressed to his fellow clergy,
with the purpose of correcting the errors of the first life. Frideswide
was probably a powerful, exceptional and active woman – she would
have to have been in order to found a community – but by the time
that Cricklade wrote his *vita* the 'ideal' of female sanctity was chastity
and chastity alone. So his account of her life concentrates on her
attempts to avoid marriage and the miraculous interventions of angels
and God that enable her to succeed. Thompson comments:

> Not only are Frideswide's activities narrowly circumscribed;
> everything in the narrative works to diminish the sense that her own
> agency is involved. Robert's description of Frideswide conspires to
> remove her from the human sphere, and the actions she performs
> are repeatedly ascribed to God's power rather than her own. When
> she speaks her words are frequently interspersed with (unattributed)
> biblical quotation which, however admirable, has the effect of making
> her seem even more inhuman.[28]

This inhumanity is further endorsed by standard evidences of
holiness: the saint learns the psalms by heart in five months, sleeps
on earth, eats no meat, and has supernatural knowledge of her
impending death. A third life is provided in *The South English
Legendary (SEL)*, which was compiled in the late thirteenth century.
Whereas Cricklade's *vita* was written in Latin for a clergy audience,
the *SEL* was written in the vernacular and aimed at the laity.
Thompson believes that it reflects the author's own experience
of rural and small urban communities where women wielded
power, because in this narrative there is little emphasis on chastity,
Frideswide is more human and more in control of her own life. *She*
makes decisions and *she* causes things to happen, not God or angels.
Her humanity is emphasized through details of her family and her
own 'interior' thoughts; less is attributed to the miraculous and more
to the saint herself. This more humane portrayal of the saint, according to Thompson, reflects a concern in the thirteenth century
with the 'science of things' as opposed to 'sciences of concepts and
definitions'; so the author of the *SEL* version looked to the lives of
women and men surrounding him to construct his narrative, whereas
Cricklade looked to hagiographic traditions and ideals.

Feminists have long maintained that patriarchy in general, of which
Christianity is a crucial part, classifies women into two categories:

virgin and whore. In the history of sainthood the repentant whore figures prominently, most clearly in the immensely popular figure of Mary Magdalen, but there is a whole array of female saints rescued from prostitution. Once again feminists hear a strong patriarchal voice in the stories of these women. In the story of Mary of Egypt, which was very popular in the Middle Ages, emphasis is placed upon the fact that this fifth-century woman chose to be a prostitute, running away from her home at the age of twelve to live in Alexandria where she enjoyed her trade so much she refused to take money from her clients. Seventeen years later she joined a ship to Jerusalem, 'seducing' every male pilgrim on the way. Once in Jerusalem she was restrained from entering the Holy Sepulchre by an invisible force until she lifted her eyes to an icon of the Blessed Virgin Mary in repentance and was told to go over the Jordan. There she lived in solitude, her worn-out clothes being replaced by lengthening hair until she was eventually discovered by a monk, Zosimus, who gave her communion and some time later found her dead and buried her with the help of a lion. In art she is depicted as carrying the three loaves she took into the desert. Feminists would draw attention to the way in which the woman is entirely responsible for her 'sin' of prostitution and is depicted as enjoying the activity. She is the one who has to repent and spend the rest of her life paying for the act. This is a standard patriarchal representation of prostitution which ignores the desperate social and economic conditions which usually drive women into a profession which they do not enjoy, and also ignores male willingness to exploit women's social and economic vulnerability. Of course it is dangerous and perhaps unfair to judge narratives composed hundreds of years ago by extremely modern standards. It is a frequent charge levelled against feminist biblical scholars and historians that they fail to appreciate the problems of judging texts and their authors by a philosophy which would be meaningless to them. However, saints and the virtues which they embody are presented to us as representing not simply the values of their age but eternal values and therefore they must be open to analysis and questioning by philosophies from different ages than their own.

Also popular in the Middle Ages and nineteenth century was the story of Thaïs, a fourth-century prostitute, also of Alexandria, who was known to murder some of her clients. A desert monk Paphnutius decided to rescue her. Having asked to talk to her somewhere other than her brothel for fear of being seen in such a place, and being reminded by the woman herself that God can see everywhere, the monk reminded her of her Christian upbringing and the horrific punishments that awaited her in the afterlife. Thaïs was converted, burnt all her clothes and jewellery and followed the monk to the desert where she was placed in a cell. Paphnutius told her: 'Your lips are too soiled to dare yet to pronounce God's name. Say only this prayer: "Thou who hast created me, have mercy on me."' For three years she was locked in this cell and fed bread and water through a hole. When she asked what she was to do about waste she was told that however bad the conditions got in her cell they were as nothing compared with what might await her in hell. After three years the monk had a vision informing him that the woman had completed her repentance. She was released into a convent and died fifteen days later. For the prostitute sainthood again lay in submitting to further male control and even violence.[29] The ideal 'whore-woman' acknowledges her sole responsibility for sinful sexual behaviour and pays for it with her life in one way or another. It is up to the holy men of God to decide when they might be suitably shriven and therefore die.

When women failed to live up to any of these ideals they were not candidates for sanctity. In particular some of the most respected women mystics (acknowledged as great in their own day and ours) who dared to venture into the 'unfeminine' realm of theology, such as Hildegard of Bingen, Julian of Norwich or some of the Beguines including Mechthild of Magdeburg, have never been formally canonized.

Mary Daly maintains that hagiography and pornography amount to the same thing, thus drawing attention to another reason why feminists have been reluctant to look at the theology of canonization. Catherine Innes-Parker illustrates the problem with reference to the Katherine Group of saints' lives written in the Middle Ages, which tell the stories of Sts Katherine of Alexandria, Margaret of Antioch and Juliana:

A young maiden is dragged into an open square, forcibly stripped, spread-eagled on the ground and beaten unmercifully. She is hung by her hair, torn with iron hooks, burned with torches, and subjected to other torments, each more hideous than the last, in full public view. Finally she is killed by the crazed madman who has ordered her public torture and humiliation. This sounds like a script for the worst kind of pornographic film. It is, in fact, a typical description of the torture of a virgin martyr as told in medieval vernacular saints' lives . . . The graphic depiction of extreme violence against women in these stories, raises the difficult question of how far these texts, often addressed specifically to women, can speak to women in an authentic way.[30]

Innes-Parker notes that the torture of virgin saints like Juliana is presented as a sexual attack, symbolic of the rape which their suitors desire. As is the case with all rape the motive is not principally sexual desire but lust to control the independent woman.

> The public exhibition of her [Juliana's] naked body and her exposure to the gaze of the onlookers and the reader becomes a kind of symbolic 'gang rape' as the torment which is prompted by Eleusius' lust becomes an expression of the lust of his men who are 'spurred' (*spurede*) on by the devil to turn the wheel by which Juliana is tortured . . . As they beat her, Eleusius' men demand that Juliana 'submit to and obey our will'.[31]

Heffernan believes that the dualistic theology of sexuality operating in Christianity lies squarely behind such disturbing narratives:

> If the body is the locus of such 'muck', why did it take centre stage in these sacred biographies? At the very foundation of such strident dualism . . . is the emotional conflict between pleasure derived from the body and the fear of the consequences of that pleasure, whether that fear has a theological or moral basis. If the congregation did receive some degree of titillation from the depiction of the sufferings of Christina or one of the other lives of the female virgins then this pleasure could only have been derived from a narrative which maltreated the desired but forbidden object, the naked maiden. Such an outlet for sexual fantasy could only obtain a public hearing by denigrating the young woman's sexuality and in so doing could instil a religiosity of shame concerning human sexuality in the congregation.[32]

Heffernan draws particular attention to the common theme in these narratives (and in modern pornography) of the mutilation of the woman's breasts. He argues that in addition to what he calls the 'erotic' element and the 'male sexual aggression' that lie behind this focus, the theological message conveyed by the mutilation of the breasts is the supernatural transformation of the woman from virgin to bride of Christ and finally to mother of Christ:

> Her breasts as the symbol of her maternity are mutilated and finally severed, to underscore the miraculous metamorphosis of the virgin into a nurturing mother, virtually a deity in her own right. The physical mutilation is also the sign of her election, as the stigmata are the authenticating sign of Christ's crucifixion.[33]

I think Heffernan's point is that the kind of mother that the woman is to become through her sainthood is spiritual rather than physical. This type of theology is based upon notions of reversal: the physical virgin becomes the spiritual bride; the breastless woman becomes the one to whom people turn to for succour. In this process the physical is devalued and dismissed.

The notion that redemption involves suffering, which lay at the heart of much medieval theology, has also come in for critical analysis by feminist theologians.[34] Although the orthodox doctrine of the atonement asserts that Christ has borne the punishment which humanity because of its sin deserves, that belief has not been taken to its logical conclusion which is that there is, therefore, no merit in suffering. On the contrary, the message has been that, so guilty should we feel for pinning Christ to the cross with our sins, and so grateful that he has taken those sins away, we should willingly suffer in imitation of him. Since Christ suffered for us, the least we can do is suffer for him, because whatever pain we might feel will be as nothing to his on that cross. Feminist theologians have been quick to pick up on the fact that the early church fathers seem to have regarded women, being children of Eve, as bearing more of the guilt for humanity's sinfulness than men and therefore in need of more self-surrender and sacrifice. Sara Maitland has provided a vivid illustration of how this imperative to suffer seems to have reached fever pitch among medieval women, at least according to hagiography:

> Women flagellate themselves, starve themselves, lacerate themselves, kiss lepers' sores (poor lepers!), deform their faces with glass, with acid, with their own fingers; they bind their limbs, carve up their bodies, pierce, bruise, cut, torture themselves. The most highly praised mystical writings use metaphorically imagery from these acts: women speak of Christ's rape of them, they abase themselves, abuse themselves . . . What the hell is going on here?[35]

We must be careful here, because hagiography may not reflect the reality of individuals' lives. But it was written for a variety of purposes, one of which was to encourage people to behave in a certain way, so even if hagiography may actually exaggerate the behaviour of certain historical women, it does send a message to all other women about what is expected of them. And, of course, these women had read or heard the graphic accounts of the sufferings of the virgin martyrs. This was how women achieved union with God. Because, unlike men, women could never escape their embodiment, their sanctity has to be won through their bodies.[36] Maitland answers her own question: what is going on is a sado-masochistic relationship with a God which 'also gives a subliminal justification to every wife-batterer, every rapist, every pornographer and every man who wishes to claim "rights", the rights to abuse, over women'.[37] Feminist theologians have noted how this glorification of suffering has had a particularly disempowering effect on women and other oppressed groups who are asked to give up that which they do not have – a sense of self. Joanne Carlson Brown and Rebecca Parker have drawn attention to the further dimension of the Son suffering at the Father's will in the traditional presentation of the doctrine of atonement, which results in 'divine child abuse' being presented as salvific.[38] Alison Webster neatly sums up the feminist analysis of the origins and implications of the Christian doctrine of atonement:

> Since men are more likely to think too much of themselves than too little, the theological emphasis has been on overcoming pride and self-importance. Self-abnegation and self-sacrifice taught in this context is somewhat different from its existential enactment in the lives of women . . . [39]

The reduction of women to two-dimensional ideals coupled with graphic descriptions of their mutilation and torture at the hands and in the sight of men are two of the obvious characteristics of pornography and so it is easy to see Daly's point. This combined with the glorification of suffering and death adds up to a feminist nightmare. Recently when I was talking with the Revd Dolores Berry, an African American pastor and gospel singer, we were discussing the feelings evoked by our visits to the tomb of Martin Luther King in Atlanta which is inscribed with the words 'Free at last! Free at last! Thank God Almighty I'm free at last.' Dolores told me that as she walked around the tomb she found herself getting angrier and angrier. At first she did not understand why, but eventually it dawned on her that she was angry because she did not want to have to die to be free as a woman, as an Afro-American and as a lesbian. But the Christian message for the past two thousand years has been exactly that: true freedom only comes at and through death and this is particularly emphasized in the lives of the female saints. Indeed, it could be said of some of the saints that they lived as if they were dead, denying themselves all of those things generally thought necessary for life. When women saints obviously internalize the theological and societal construction of woman through their own writings or reported words, then they become even less appealing to today's Christian feminists. Salt is rubbed into the wound by the way particularly impressive women are often credited in hagiography with having lost their femaleness altogether and achieved the heights of manliness. Gillian Cloke who has studied this phenomenon notes:

> We have example after example of women applauded for this capacity; the striking thing about the reports of pious women of the fourth to fifth centuries is how uniformly their virtue is judged in the context of their sex rather than set in a background of Christian achievements of their area or age in general . . . When fourth century church writers considered the virtuous woman they would invariably refer to her sex, only to set her apart from it . . . There was a connection at something like visceral level for the Christian writers of the ancient world between virtue and masculinity . . . So the property of virtue pertains to being like a man . . . [40]

It was therefore the ultimate compliment for a saintly woman to be referred to as 'manly'. Palladius referred to Melania the Elder as 'the female man of God' and there are hundreds of examples of women earning this 'ultimate' title from admiring men.

Having examined some of the ways in which female saints are presented in hagiography – and not just hagiography of the distant past – one can begin to appreciate why feminists have not shown much interest in sainthood. It is also possible to sympathize with the verdict of Cardinal Newman (himself a candidate for canonization) on saints' lives: 'They do not manifest a Saint, they mince him into spiritual lessons.'[41] There are other reasons for this reluctance, some theological, but before turning to these it is necessary to consider the process of canonization because this also grates with the philosophy and practice of feminism.

The process of stealing souls

The term 'canonization' first appears in Western literature in the eleventh century and it was only from the twelfth century that the word began to be regularly applied to the process of declaring someone a saint. The word comes from the Greek *kanonizein*, meaning to regularize or authorize. It also refers to the practice of inserting the saint's name into the canon of the Mass. In earliest Christianity the term 'saint' (*hagios* in Greek) was applied to the whole Christian community and its individual members. Then it came to be applied to distinct individuals, bishops, priests, virgins and abbesses, whether living or dead, whose holiness was believed to be 'above average'. But it quickly acquired the meaning it still has today. The process of declaring a dead person to be a saint, to have a holiness beyond that of ordinary Christians which earns them immediate access to paradise, began as a purely popular reaction to the death of the early Christian martyrs. Their relics and tombs were venerated, and the practice later spread to 'confessors' who suffered but did not die in persecution, and then in the fourth century to 'virgins', these too being believed to have achieved the status of the martyrs after their death and to have privileged powers of intercession with God. This belief in the privileged position of martyrs had its roots in post-exilic Judaism. Local bishops and the synods over which they presided quickly moved to take some sort of control of Christian practice to prevent veneration of people they defined as heretics. When cults of particular saints began to spread beyond confined areas, and as part of the general centralization of power in Rome in Western Christendom, the papacy attempted to take complete control of the regulation of cults. This was achieved by the thirteenth century, by which time a formal process had developed and was formalized, incorporating evidence of sanctity, miracles, the support of local bishop and plenary council, and eyewitness accounts.[42] All this was to establish whether the candidate measured up to the three characteristics of sainthood: a person who (a) has led a life of heroic virtue; (b) has gone to heaven; (c) is a legitimate object of public devotion. It was also in the medieval period that a distinction began to be drawn between beatification and canonization. Persons who are beatified may be venerated only within a particular location (a particular diocese or religious order); a canonized person is venerated universally. Seven honours came to be accorded to a saint: (a) their names were put in the official catalogues of saints; (b) public intercession might be made to them; (c) churches could be dedicated to their memory; (d) the Eucharist and divine office could be celebrated in their honour; (e) their festival was observed universally; (f) they could be represented pictorially in devotional art; (g) their relics were enclosed in special vessels and venerated. The centralization of the process of canonization had several repercussions. One was that the lives (*vitae*) of the saints became much more explicitly tools in the canonization process: lives were written for the purpose of getting someone approved by the 'system'. They therefore had to demonstrate that the candidate exhibited all the right qualities and had done all the right things, hence they could become rather stylized. The second repercussion was that saints became, much more overtly than previously, part of ecclesiastical politics. Their lives became vehicles for the dominant theology, morality and political culture.

(This close connection between saints and culture is evident in the fluctuating popularity of saints. The Victorian preoccupation with the rescue of 'fallen' women led to the popular revival of not only Mary Magdalen but also long-forgotten ex-prostitutes from the patristic era.) The centralization of canonization also had an effect upon who ultimately passed the test. Saints became mirrors of the changing values of European society, both in terms of the people who were made saints and in terms of the ways in which their lives were shaped.[43]

Not only was the canonization process part of the political manoeuvrings in the Church and society: so also was the potency of saints' relics. Areas did battle for relics because relics brought prestige, pilgrims and money. Very early on, bishops like Augustine had to deal with the problem of wealthy families acquiring the bodies of martyrs and using them in various ways to familial advantage. But the saints could also be used to direct behaviour in an immediate way. Patrick Geary has described the ritual of the 'humiliation of the saints' used in the Middle Ages by clergy seeking to exercise control over the laity. In a dispute with the laity, guardians of saintly relics would 'humiliate' the relics, placing them upon the ground in the middle of the Mass, so making the grievance clear; and there the relics would stay until the dispute was resolved. 'In a sense, the monks or canons went on strike from their primary task of providing local access and proper veneration to Christ and the saints . . . Right or wrong, their opponent and the rest of society could not endure the mistreatment of its defenders and patrons for ever.'[44] Not only were the people cut off from their patrons, but the humiliated saints were expected to seek retribution for their humiliation. The abuse of the power of sainthood was one of the targets of the Reformers. In 1520 Luther wrote a tract parodying the relic collection of one archbishop: 'a fine piece of the left horn of Moses, three flames from the bush of Moses on Mount Sinai, two feathers and an egg from the Holy Ghost, an entire corner of the banner with which Christ rose from Hell.' This parody was particularly sharp because the actual collection claimed to contain one of Judas' silver pieces, some crumbs of manna from the desert, a piece of earth on which Jesus stood when teaching his followers the 'Our Father', two vats from Cana and a piece of a miraculous cloak which Mary made for Jesus and which expanded as he grew! The Reformers also found the merit system that surrounded the saints unscriptural and abusable by the Church hierarchy.

Weinstein and Bell have analysed trends in canonization since the process came under papal control. They discovered that between the thirteenth and sixteenth centuries most of the saints made were Italian and urban and their principal virtue was a heroic struggle to maintain their chastity. They gave expression to the 'intense moral and spiritual anxieties of the urban middle classes'.[45] An early sociological study of the saints in all ages concluded that 78 per cent were what twentieth-century Westerners would label 'upper class', of royal or noble blood, 17 per cent were middle class and only 5 per cent were 'lower class', i.e. of peasant stock. There is a tendency in hagiography for the social status of the male saint to rise (but never fall); for women saints, their social status does sometimes fall.[46] Although percentages vary from century to century the trend remains remarkably stable. The trend is also clear regarding gender, with women accounting for no more than 28 per cent of saints in the period of Weinstein and Bell's study.[47] They point out that part of the Roman Catholic Church's response to the Protestant Reformation was to reaffirm the role of the hierarchical male in the Church, by clearly endorsing episcopal and clerical authority and by emphasizing the importance of the sacraments which of course were celebrated by a male priesthood; this was reflected in the sort of people made saints. In 1988, of the 1,369 active causes for canonization on the Vatican's lists, still only 20 per cent were lay.[48] From the twelfth century onwards those women who did make it into the canon tended to be founders of religious orders, and this remains true in our own age. Between 1965 and 1975, 62 people were canonized by Rome, including the Forty Martyrs of England and Wales; eight of the 22 canonized as individuals were women who founded religious orders. No lay non-martyrs made the grade. Cunningham has remarked: 'One could argue, with a certain whimsical edge, that a quick perusal of the Church calendar of saints would lead one to define a modern saint as any conspicuously pious European who happens to have founded a new religious order after the Reformation.'[49]

Periodically the system of canonization was reformed, but every time this happened power seemed to be more centralized and the variety of saints diminished. In the early eighteenth century the canon lawyer Prospero Lorenzo Lambertini, who was deeply involved in the process of canonization, published an extensive study on the subject, tracing its history but also seeking to clarify the necessary stages and evidence.[50] Lambertini, who later became Benedict XIV, fashioned the long, judicial process of canonization that existed until 1983. This could only begin 50 years after the subject's death and focused (but only in its fourth stage) on the figures of the Postulator of the cause and the Promoter of the Faith (popularly known as the devil's advocate).[51] These two magisterial officials battled sometimes for decades against each other through the medium of documentation, and if successful the case went through several judicial reviews by the Congregation of Rites (which became in 1969 the Congregation for the Causes of Saints) until all, including the Pope, were satisfied as to the holiness and orthodoxy of the candidate. Then the Pope declared the candidate to be a 'venerable'. Pope Pius XI introduced a further stage at this point in 1920. Called the 'historical section', its purpose was to investigate the historical evidence around those candidates whose contemporaries had died. Then the corpse was exhumed and examined for identification purposes. If the body was found to be incorrupt, this could be used as evidence of sanctity (a sign of the saint's achievement in transcending the normal but sinful and impure processes of the body). Then miracles were examined. Miracles had to be of such a quality as to prove that God had performed them and it had to be proved that the miracle occurred through the intervention of the would-be saint. This evidence was gathered by the local bishop, who initially responded to the petitioners requesting him to open the official cause of the saint, although the evidence was reassessed by judges appointed by the Holy See. The evidence was then sent to Rome to be subjected to the Promoter and Postulator, theological and medical experts were consulted and several meetings of the Congregation were held, and eventually the Pope certified the acceptance of the miracles and issued a final decree. Then two further verified miracles were needed before beatification could take place, and two more miracles before canonization (although martyrs were not required to produce the same degree of miraculous proof as non-martyrs). If these materialized the candidate was beatified at a solemn Mass, at which the Pope did not officiate, and canonized at a solemn Mass at which the Pope did. This complex and extremely lengthy process, designed to prevent abuses and embarrassing mistakes, also made the process less politically malleable, although as the case of Goretti indicates it was possible to 'rush through' certain canonizations if necessary.

In 1983 John Paul II subjected the canonization process to what everyone agreed was a long overdue revision. The judicial model was replaced by an academic one; the office of the Promoter of the Faith was abolished. A college of relators was established to supervise the writing of a historical account of the candidate and a prelate theologian was charged with choosing the theological consultors for each stage of the process. The whole system has been simplified dramatically, with much of the work being done locally without replication in Rome (although Rome still has to ratify the candidate's orthodoxy). The Roman stage is far less disputatious and generally more positive. The number of miracles needed at each stage has been halved. Despite the fact that most of the key posts in the process are now technically open to lay men and women, the holders of the offices remain overwhelmingly male and clerical. Despite the reforms of the system the cost is exorbitant and most of it has to be met by the original petitioners. This has resulted in an over-representation of founders of religious orders in the catalogue of saints, since these institutions tend to have the necessary funds. Pope John Paul II has used the system he reformed to push through beatifications and canonizations at what some have claimed to be an indecent pace. The women he has beatified and canonized have generally conformed to the standard types – virgins, martyrs, founders.

Enormous disquiet has been expressed over his support of the cause of Edith Stein, some accusing the Pope of using this woman as a means of deflecting attention away from the Catholic Church's accommodations with the Nazi regime. Stein (1891–1942) was Jewish by birth but by the age of fifteen regarded herself as an atheist and a feminist. She had a brilliant scholarly mind and at university studied philosophy under Edmund Husserl the phenomenologist. She also became close friends with Husserl's colleague Adolph Reinach who was a Roman Catholic. The strength shown by Reinach's widow when he was killed, and an introduction to the works of Teresa of Avila impressed Stein and in 1922 she converted to Catholicism. She became a teacher and writer, becoming a popular speaker on Catholic philosophy, yet she also felt she had a vocation to become a Carmelite. In 1933, when as a person of Jewish extraction she could no longer teach, she was finally accepted as a postulant, taking the name Sister Theresa Benedicta. Stein undoubtedly became more aware of her own Jewishness at this point and wrote to Pius XI urging him to do something about the plight of Jews in Germany, but she also offered firstly her cloistered life and then her sufferings for atonement on behalf of the Jewish people and in the hope that they would be led to the Catholic Church. In 1938 the situation had become so unsafe in Germany for Stein, and for her fellow sisters who might be accused of sheltering Jews, that she left her convent in Cologne and went to one in Echt in Holland. In 1942 the Roman Catholic bishops of Holland spoke out, condemning the deportation of Holland's Jewish people. The Nazis retaliated by rounding up all the Jewish members of Dutch religious orders and deporting them to concentration camps. Stein eventually ended up in Auschwitz and was gassed. The canonization process had to prove that Stein died, not 'just' for being a Jew, but for her Christian faith, as this is the only grounds for declaring someone a martyr, and the absence of miracles and a body meant that martyrdom was the only option. It was eventually decided that Stein died because of the stand of the bishops of Holland. In 1987 she was unprecedentedly declared both a martyr and a confessor. Members of her order caused offence to Jews over many years by setting up a convent in the grounds of Auschwitz with papal approval.

Stein's cause betrays many of the characteristics that make a lot of people, not only feminists, unhappy with the process of canonization: the growth in ecumenical and multi-faith consciousness within the Roman Catholic Church does not seem to have touched the canonization process. The offence that the promotion of Stein's canonization causes to many Jews is simply ignored, as are arguments which first began to be formulated in the 1960s in the wake of Vatican II for the opening up of the process to include non-Catholics, like Dietrich Bonhoeffer and Martin Luther King, and non-Christians such as Gandhi.[52] The Church may no longer declare that 'outside the Church there is no salvation', but this is not borne out in its lists of saints. The canonization process is one of the many indications, but perhaps the clearest, that at the end of the twentieth century the Vatican is little changed except perhaps in a few externals from the Vatican of the beginning of the twentieth century.

Reforms in the canonization process have done nothing to calm the disquiet of ecumenists, those involved in inter-faith dialogue, or feminists. Pope Paul's contribution was to reform the liturgical calendar. In the spirit of Vatican II he felt that the calendar had become so full that the 'principal mysteries of redemption' had become obscured in the liturgical life of the Church. Under Paul the veneration of saints was simplified, with the vast majority of saints being commemorated by optional 'Memorials', rather than by 'Feasts', which commemorate the biblical saints and a few others, and 'Solemnities', which are the most important holy days and are celebrated with a vigil the night before. Only the Blessed Virgin Mary, and Sts Joseph, John the Baptist, Peter and Paul and All Saints'

Day qualify for this honour. A host of saints was removed from the calendar altogether, ostensibly because their existence was histori- cally doubtful, and devotion to other saints was confined to specific areas (e.g. geographic areas or religious orders), but saints were also added to the calendar.[53] Many male saints were scrapped, including a number of canonized Popes, but also erased were some of the most well-known women saints of history whose cults had enjoyed prominence particularly among women; these included Sts Katherine of Alexandria and Margaret of Antioch. Katherine and Margaret were two of a list of saints known as Fourteen Holy Helpers or Auxiliary Saints who enjoyed a collective cult in northern Europe from the fourteenth century onwards. There were three women in these fourteen, the third being St Barbara. When the calendar was reformed in 1969 the cults of these women (including Barbara) were suppressed completely. Only one of the male saints had his cult suppressed – St Eustace. Two of the others had their cult reduced from a universal to a purely local one – Sts George and Christopher – and the rest were left unscathed, despite the fact that the historical evidence for most of them is questionable and no more or less questionable than for the women concerned. The reform of the calendar did not lessen the racial or gender imbalance. Two-thirds of the saints in the reformed calendar (discounting those mentioned in the Bible) were European and one-third of them were Italian. Only 24 non-biblical women were included; the majority were virgins and founders of religious orders, two (Perpetua and Felicity) were martyrs, one was the mother of a saint – St Monica – and one was a queen (Margaret of Scotland, who played a large part in Romanizing the Church in Scotland). Only nine of the male saints were neither clergy nor religious, and they were by and large royal.[54]

Considering all the negative aspects of canonization (the process, its use for political ends and the way that women saints are represented) it is little wonder that many in our own day have lost confidence in the process and are reluctant even to try to promote the causes of those who do not fit the Vatican's stereotypes. This is clearly illustrated by the case of Dorothy Day (1897–1980). This remarkable woman was a convert to Catholicism who never felt entirely comfortable with the Church. She took vows of poverty, chastity and obedience but held to them very loosely. She was orthodox in doctrinal belief but was never controlled by the Church, never flinching from criticizing the hierarchy whenever it did anything that might harm the disadvantaged. She was a political activist and socialist who co-founded (with Peter Maurin) the Catholic Worker movement and journal which sought to build a new society based upon the philosophy of the Sermon on the Mount. She was a champion of the poor and workers' rights, founding a network of homes for the destitute. She resolutely discouraged any adulation in her own lifetime. She was devoted to three women saints – Catherine of Siena, Teresa of Avila and Thérèse of Lisieux – but believed that sanctity was something to which all Christians were called. She knew that someone would try and promote her cause after her death and this worried her for two reasons. She was acutely aware that she did not fit any 'ideals', she knew herself to be extremely human; before her conversion she had been sexually involved with a number of men, she had been divorced, had a child out of wedlock and had had an abortion. Nor had her conversion wiped away her tendency to bad temper or judgementalism. She did not want details of her private life scrutinized in the process of canonization. But she was also aware of what the Church did to saints and once declared 'Don't call me a saint! I don't want to be dismissed so easily!' However, a couple of years after her death the Claretian Fathers of Chicago did begin the process. Day's own relatives discouraged them, suggesting that the money (Woodward has estimated that it costs at least $100,000 for a person to be canonized[55]) would be better used in service of the people to whom Day dedicated her life. This opinion was shared by her fellow activist Fr Daniel Berrigan SJ. He wrote of the possible promotion of her cause:

> Dorothy is a people's saint, she was careful and proud of her dignity as a lay person. Her poverty of spirit, a great gift to our age, would forbid the expensive puffing of baroque sainthood. Today her spirit haunts us in the violated faces of the homeless of New York. Can you imagine her portrait, all gussied up, unfurled from above the high altar of St Peter's? I say, let them go on canonising canons and such. We have here a saint whose soul ought not be stolen from her people – the wretched of the earth.[56]

This is perhaps the gravest indictment of the canonization process in the Roman Church, that it 'steals the souls' of those whom it chooses to adopt. No doubt many Vatican officials would be highly suspicious of Day anyway, but it is interesting that her family and friends see the process of canonization in entirely negative terms.

Of course the Roman Catholic Church has long acknowledged that it does not have knowledge of all the saints who enjoy communion with God. Hence the early institution (seventh century at the latest) of All Saints' Day, a feast to celebrate all saints known and *unknown*. Yet by claiming the sole right and privilege of canonization the Vatican claims knowledge of what kind of person is (and therefore by default what kind of person is not) 'holy', i.e. acceptable in the sight of God. Saint-making is perhaps the most effective form of theo-logical communication in the Church because it concretizes, indeed incarnates, the ideology dominating at the time. Lives make much better reading or watching than apostolic letters or theological treatises and they reach more people. It is also more difficult to argue against a life: one can attack intellectual propositions with integrity but to attack a canonization can be interpreted as attacking a life, a person. What has become increasingly obvious is that the centre of power in the Roman Catholic Church uses saint-making as a way of making visible, of manifesting, its own theology in the most indisputable way possible.

The Roman Catholic Church is not the only church to have saints or to reserve the right to make saints. The Orthodox family of churches also canonizes. As in the Roman Church, the history of canonization has been a history of gradual centralization, from popular acclaim to local bishops to Metropolitans, although the process took a lot longer. The Orthodox Churches also place less emphasis on individual saints and more emphasis on the communion of saints than Rome. Eva Catafygiotu Topping has made a study of the presentation of Orthodox female saints, most of whom are ignored in the liturgy. Her study reveals very similar parallels with the Roman manipulation and presentation of women saints.[57]

No more heroes anymore

Feminists may also have theological reasons for having little interest in the concept of sainthood. Central to feminist theology and to womanist, *mujerista* and all other forms of feminist theological reflection is the notion that liberating power is focused not in hierarchical systems but in relationships and community based upon mutuality – some have named this power erotic power or passion and it is fundamentally expressed in friendship.[58] Elisabeth Schüssler Fiorenza has done an enormous amount of work on the 'patriarchal-ization of the discipleship-community of equals',[59] arguing that in origin the Jesus-movement was decidedly subversive of patriarchal structures, replacing the corner-stone of patriarchy – the family – with new understandings of kinship in which there were no fathers, only friends. It is this vision which feminist theology seeks to make real again in our own day. Part of this project involves the exposure and deconstruction of the patriarchal basis of much Christian doctrine. Rita Nakashima Brock tackled the central doctrine of christology and some of her insights may cast light on the patriarchal basis of much of the theology of sainthood. She argues that the focusing of notions of transformation/salvation on the one person of Jesus reflects 'an androcentric preoccupation with heroes'.[60] The hero is part of the patriarchal familial model of the way the world works. Male figures at the apex of the pyramid control the lives of those who form layers of hierarchy below them and those at the base are dependent upon those who occupy the higher echelons. We have already touched on the difficulties feminists have had with atonement christologies, in which the Father demands that the Son/hero suffers on behalf of the masses in order that wounded relationships be healed. In traditional theologies of sainthood the saints become heroes close to the top of the apex of the pyramid, and they have had to suffer to 'earn' that place, in order to intercede on behalf of the helpless ones at the base. Such a theology is profoundly disempowering to the majority, rendering them dependent. Saints simply occupy another rung on the hierarchical ladder and even though some may be female, the splendid isolation of those who have attained this status, their unique-ness and éliteness and our dependence upon them, is antithetical to a vision of mutuality, community and friendship. Indeed, it could be argued that the presence of female saints serves in some way to mask the patriarchal dynamics at work.

It is fascinating to read of the visions that Perpetua and her fellow martyr Saturus had before their death. These included a vision of their reception into the heavenly court after their deaths, obviously based very closely on Daniel 7. In the vision they find themselves before the throne of 'one like unto a man white-haired' with the face of a youth. Four angels lift the two martyrs up to the figure 'and we kissed him, and he stroked our face with his hand. And the other elders said to us, "Let us stand". And we stood and gave the kiss of peace. And the elders said to us, "Go and play".'[61] The scene is one of small children with their distant parent, almost the perfect carica-ture of the Victorian father. Because they have been 'good children' and given their lives for him they are petted and sent out to 'play'. Saints are often represented as children before God in medieval art. And, as Thomas Heffernan has pointed out, in some medieval hagiography the virginal female martyr is transformed into the heavenly mother and mediatrix.[62] Thus the family pyramid is built up and secured, and now those left behind become like small children petitioning the saint for gracious favours. The feudal model of divine reality that dominated Christianity ensured that saints not only functioned as intercessors, but had power in their own right which they dispensed at will. Although the scholastic theologians made clear distinctions between the worship (*latria*) due only to God and the veneration (*dulia*) due to the saints, and veneration of the saints has never been declared necessary for salvation, yet because saints offered a human face to divine reality their power was enormous and therefore so was the power of those who fashioned them.

Carter Heyward, in her study of erotic or passionate power, reinforces the need to work towards what she calls 'right relation' and honestly acknowledge and deal with factors which obstruct the formation of that right relation. She acknowledges that we all need help to sustain the 'staying power' necessary to foster and maintain right relationship amidst structures which are antithetical to it but she is quite clear that what we need is friends, not heroes:

> Heroes show us who we are *not*. Helpers show us who we *are*. As individual supermen/wonderwomen, heroes diminish our senses of relational, or shared, power. Helpers call us forth into our power in relation and strengthen our senses of ourselves. Heroes have brought us 'religion' in many forms . . . They have brought us 'solutions' (that is what heroes are for) . . . Heroes have brought us causes and crusades, flags and battles, soldiers and bombs. As our liberators and leaders, popes and presidents, bishops and priests, shrinks and teachers, mentors and gurus, heroes have brought us pipedreams and smokescreens and everything but salvation. And this, I am persuaded, is because we tend to search everywhere except among ourselves-in-relation for peace.[63]

Heyward also makes the point with regard to standard human heroes that has already been made regarding saintly ones, that when we romanticize them we 'render one-dimensional that which has many dimensions'. She argues that romanticizing people trivializes both them and us and 'to romanticize is to idealize; it is to trivialize by ignoring completely' It could be argued on the basis of evidence surveyed earlier in this chapter that women saints are prime examples of how the process and theology of canonization has rendered women one-dimensional and by romanticizing certain qualities, attributes or actions has trivialized their lives and those of all women.

It is only too obvious how the saints show us who we are not. Indeed, at the heart of sainthood is a comparison between superior and 'standard' notions of holiness. The 'solution' that these heroes offer is to the problem of a paterfamilias God, the image of the divine moulded in and by the patriarchal process in Christianity 'beyond', 'above' and 'other', so distant from the base of the pyramid as to be invisible, to be only 'heard about' from those closer to the apex – and taking his son with him. The saints became the human face of the heavenly court, the friendly recognizable faces at reception who had access to whatever lay behind the solid doors or mysterious curtains, or the kind and reassuring lawyers who would represent you in court before the judge. They had feet in both worlds and so could relate to both, the perfect go-betweens. This image of a distant, other God is one that feminist theologians, among others, have strenuously fought against, since it reflects and bolsters the male patriarchal pyramid in society as a whole and in the Church in particular. In feminist theology the divine is close and yet also beyond our control, in our midst yet unwilling to be pinned down. Heyward in her discussion of christology has argued that the clear and fundamental distinction between humanity and divinity in classic Christian theology is itself a manifestation of and expression of the dualism that has haunted Christianity to the detriment of women and others.[64] She locates the presence of the divine in erotic power/right relationship, in the midst of the struggle for mutuality and community. There is therefore no room in her theology for any kind of doctrine of election, as she noted in a sermon preached on All Saints' Day, 1983.

> The doctrine of 'election', however interpreted, can be postulated only on an assumption that God has chosen certain people and not others to participate in the 'mystical' body of Christ. Why must our faith rest on the grounds of exclusivity and special privilege? More to the point, *can* our faith stand on these grounds? I believe not. Our God, the One whom Jesus loved, does not pick and choose, select, elect, set apart, lift up certain groups of people, or individuals, to be 'godlike' or 'saintly'. God chose us all, Christians and Jews and Moslems and wicca, and other so-called pagan peoples of all races and nations; both genders, men and women who are single, married, lesbian, gayman, heterosexual, celibate, sexually active; in good health and in poor health. God continues to choose us all. We are the ones who elect, select, sort out, and decide in relation to one another where we shall stand and how we shall live as members of this mystical body. This is a very real and very present body of all people, those who have died, and those who are still alive in this world.[65]

Feminist theology, therefore, has real problems with some of the central notions that appear to lie behind the Christian notion of saint-hood – the creation of heroes and élites with particular privileges and powers within the Christian community. Not only is this practice antithetical to feminist theory, but Christian feminists like Heyward maintain it is antithetical to the gospel vision itself.

The basic qualification

'In the first place, a saint is either a corpse or part of one. The world has no use for living saints, they are dead persons, or still better – the potency of the dead.'[66] It is a truism to state that to be a saint is to be dead. Certainly there are people whom others acclaim to be living saints (like Mother Teresa) during their lifetime but the very words '*living* saints' indicate that in the popular mentality, and certainly in the official teaching of the Church, a saint is someone who has to be dead. Jane Stevenson, in concluding her analysis of early Irish saints, offers a explanation for this basic requirement:

> This is what early medieval Ireland expected. A saint should be a mighty curser, a tireless ascetic, a wonderworker, a prophet and seer, and indefatigable guardian of his rights, lands and treasures. He should not be a mere mortal, transcending the limits of the human condition by sheer force of will. Thus, the powerful drive to project a fantasy of power on to the concept of sanctity meant that, in practice, the only good saint was one who had been dead long enough to have been completely forgotten.[67]

Death is essential to make the saint mouldable, it is part of the idealization process.

It has previously been pointed out that declaring someone a saint is in a large measure a declaration that they are certainly enjoying union with God/gone to heaven. Mary Daly has constantly accused Christianity of being 'necrophiliac', focused as it appears to be on the cross and on life after death. Feminist theology, Christian and post-Christian, has tended to be highly suspicious of the theology of life after death, believing it to be part of the scourge of dualism which pits body and soul, woman and man, humanity and deity, life and death against one another. Rosemary Radford Ruether has listed belief in an individual afterlife as one of the dualisms we have to ditch if we are to survive the ecological crisis intact.

Human bodies are finite organisms, centres of experience, which also decay, fall into organic waste and are to be composted back into the nexus of matter to rise again as new organic forms. And what of our consciousness, what we have called our souls? I think this is not separable from this same process of disintegration, extinguished with our distinct mortal organisms and entering again into the well of dependent origination.[68]

Feminists are also well aware of how hope in life after death has been used in Christianity to encourage people into passively accepting situations of oppression in the present in the belief that by doing so they are earning 'pie in the sky when they die'. Concern with individual eternal destiny also isolates the individual from the community of which he/she is a part and for which she/he is responsible. It helps to breed notions of independence and absolute autonomy which liberation and feminist theologians believe are at least partly responsible for the divisions in our societies and the destruction of our environment.

Daphne Hampson, a post-Christian feminist, has suggested that the search for immortality is a particularly male concern. Drawing on the work of Carol Gilligan she suggests the obsession with life after death reflects male psychology. Gilligan found that men were more isolated than women, with a much greater sense of an autonomous, independent self; they tend to see the world in relationship to themselves and feel they have to master it, make an impression upon it. Women tend to see themselves in terms of relationships with others; therefore it should come as no surprise that the preoccupation of continued individual existence after death is a preoccupation of male religion. Hampson cites the thoughts of Charlotte Perkins Gilman on this issue:

> To the death-based religion, the main question is, 'What is going to happen to me after I am dead?' – a posthumous egotism. To the birth-based religion, the main question is, 'What must be done for the child who is born?' an immediate altruism . . . The death-based religions have led to a limitless individualism, a demand for the eternal extension of personality. Such good conduct as they required was to placate the deity or to benefit one's self . . . The birth-based religion is necessarily and essentially altruistic, a forgetting of oneself for the good of the child, and tends to develop naturally into love and labour for the widening range of family, state and world.[69]

Both Gilligan and Anne Wilson Schaef found in their analysis of the psychology of the different sexes that men's concern with immortality far outweighed that of women. Women's concern is with maintaining a network of relations in this life and ensuring that it is possible for those who come after to live in conditions where such relationships are possible. Hampson cites Carol Christ, who believes that preoccupation with belief in life after death has contributed to the way in which humankind remained unconcerned about exploiting the earth and her resources:

> The knowledge that we could destroy this earth weighs heavily on me . . . I can imagine my own death and do not really fear it . . . We must learn to love this life that ends in death. This is not absolutely to rule out the possibility of individual or communal survival after death, but to say that we ought not to live our lives in the light of such a possibility. Our task is here . . . The spirituality we need for our survival, I would argue, is precisely a spirituality encouraging us to recognise limitation and mortality, a spirituality calling us to celebrate all that is finite.[70]

One could argue that the doctrine of sainthood as it has emerged reflects the male hope or even conviction that the next life for which they long will be a mirror of this, with a clear hierarchy and that in the gentlemen's club (with lady associate members, of course) there are already old boys (and girls) on the governing committee who can use their influence to get you membership and smooth your path to the door.

Miracles

Feminists are suspicious of the emphasis upon 'miracle' in Christianity in general and the lives of the saints in particular. The disruption of natural processes by divine intervention again assumes a dualistic relationship between divinity and humanity, deity and matter. As manifest in the lives of the saints it may reflect again a preoccupation with and desire to gain ultimate control over our environment and to be able to bend it according to human will. And again it creates situations of dependence and élitism.

The word 'canon' in origin referred to a measuring rod or ruler. It is understandable why feminist theologians have chosen implicitly to dismiss the theology of sainthood and canonization as a patriarchal tool designed to measure humanity by the rule of patriarchal male consciousness. I have deliberately painted a 'worst case scenario' in this chapter to draw out all the elements of canonization that offend feminist theory, theology and practice. I have, as it were, overturned the bin and poured out all the rubbish. I take this metaphor from Ruether who, inspired by Catherine Keller's observation that feminists are the great recyclers of culture, suggested that feminists are like 'Filipino orphans sifting through the great mountains of trash abandoned by destructive social systems and trying to recover useable bits and pieces from which to construct a new habitation'.[71] As Ruether goes on to point out, this 'grim' image actually conveys important facets of the feminist theologian's task: it indicates that there is much of the past that is usable but only if it is handled with a new vision and shaped into new forms that reflect that vision, and women must be responsible for that reconstruction. The rubbish has been tipped on the floor – why not walk away from it? Some can and do and find other piles with what they believe to be better material for reconstruction, but I share Elisabeth Schüssler Fiorenza's belief that 'Catholic women cannot simply turn away from the images and cult of the saints without paying the price of alienation from ourselves and from our particular Christian tradition and community'. By refusing to engage with our saintly inheritance, 'we are in danger of leaving these religious images of women in command and control of Catholic women's psyche, not to mention in the command and control of the male hierarchy which interprets their meaning for women'.[72] And as Margaret Miles has pointed out, if we concentrate only upon the oppression of women in and by history 'we will miss the creativity with which women – never the primary shapers of their cultures – have foraged in their cultural environment for the tools with which they make their lives'.[73] And not only Catholics are involved in this process: most Christian denominations have some concept of sainthood. And it is precisely because these women saints are appealed to and indeed are still being created by the male hierarchy that it is essential for feminists to dive into the rubbish and start reclaiming, recycling and reforming.

NOTES

1 Elisabeth Schüssler Fiorenza, *Discipleship of Equals: A Critical Feminist Ekklesia-logy of Liberation* (London: SCM, 1993), p. 40.
2 Giordano Bruno Guerri, 'Poor Assassin: Poor Saint: The True Story of Maria Goretti': see Kenneth L. Woodward, *Making Saints Inside the Vatican: Who Became Saints, Who Do Not and Why* (London: Chatto and Windus, 1991), pp. 123–4.

3 Ann Ball, *Modern Saints: Their Lives and Faces* (Rockford: Tan Books, 1983), p. 163.
4 Brother Kenneth CGA, *Saints of the Twentieth Century* (London: Mowbray, 1987), p. 110.
5 Ball, *Modern Saints*, p. 183.
6 Ball, *Modern Saints*, p. 184.
7 Ball, *Modern Saints*, p. 185.
8 Carol J. Adams, 'Naming, denial and sexual violence', *Miriam's Song*, vol. 5, p. 21.
9 Eva Catafygiotu Topping, *Holy Mothers of Orthodoxy* (Minneapolis: Light and Life, 1987), p. 3.
10 Donald Weinstein and Rudolf M. Bell, *Saints and Society: The Two Worlds of Western Christendom, 1000–1700* (Chicago: University of Chicago Press, 1982), p. 87.
11 Thomas J. Heffernan, *Sacred Biography: Saints and Their Biographers in the Middle Ages* (Oxford: Oxford University Press, 1988), p. 278.
12 Sara Maitland, 'Passionate prayer: masochistic images in women's experience' in Linda Hurcombe (ed.), *Sex and God: Some Varieties of Women's Religious Experience* (London: Routledge, 1987), p. 130.
13 Eamon Duffy, 'Holy maydens, holy wyfes: the cult of women saints in fifteenth and sixteenth-century England' in W. J. Sheils and Diana Wood (eds), *Women in the Church: Papers Read at the 1989 Summer Meeting and the 1990 Winter Meeting of the Ecclesiastical History Society* (Oxford: Basil Blackwell, 1990), pp. 175–96.
14 Woodward, *Making Saints*, p. 341.
15 Maitland, 'Passionate prayer', p. 134.
16 Maitland, 'Passionate prayer', pp. 134–5.
17 Maitland, 'Passionate prayer', p. 136.
18 Since the Middle Ages certain theologians regarded as outstanding and saintly have been given the title 'Doctor of the Church'. Originally the title was confined to four: Ambrose, Augustine, Jerome and Gregory the Great, but the list was extended and now over thirty people bear the title.
19 From Rhigyfarch's *Life* of David cited in Patrick Thomas, *Candle in the Darkness: Celtic Spirituality from Wales* (Llandysul: Gomer Press, 1993), p. 112.
20 St Augustine, *Confessions: Translation and with an Introduction and Notes by Henry Chadwick* (Oxford: Oxford University Press, 1991), p. 168.
21 St Augustine, *Confessions*, pp. 168–9.
22 Clarissa W. Atkinson, ' "Your servant, my mother": the figure of Saint Monica in the ideology of Christian motherhood' in Clarissa W. Atkinson, Constance H. Buchanan and Margaret R. Miles, *Immaculate and Powerful: The Female in Sacred Image and Social Reality* (Boston: Beacon Press, 1985), pp. 139–72.

23 Atkinson, '"Your servant, my mother"', p. 162.
24 Sean Kelly and Rosemary Rogers, *Saints Preserve Us!* (London: Robson Books, 1995), p. 206.
25 Elissa R. Henken, *Traditions of the Welsh Saints* (Cambridge: D. S. Brewer, 1987) and *The Welsh Saints: A Study in Pattern Lives* (Cambridge: D. S. Brewer, 1991).
26 Susan Haskins, *Mary Magdalen: Myth and Metaphor* (London: HarperCollins, 1993).
27 Marina Warner, *Joan of Arc: The Image of Female Heroism* (London: Vintage, 1991).
28 Anne Thompson, 'Shaping a saint's Life: Frideswide of Oxford', *Medium Aevum*, vol. 63, no. 1 (1994), p. 39.
29 Benedicta Ward, *Signs and Wonders: Saints, Miracles and Prayers from the Fourth Century to the Fourteenth* (Aldershot: Variorum, 1992), pp. 39–49.
30 Catherine Innes-Parker, 'Sexual violence and the female reader: symbolic "rape" in the saints' lives of the Katherine group', *Women's Studies*, vol. 24, no. 3 (1995), p. 205.
31 Innes-Parker, 'Sexual violence and the female reader', pp. 207–8.
32 Heffernan, *Sacred Biography*, p. 282.
33 Heffernan, *Sacred Biography*, p. 283.
34 See Rita Nakashima Brock, *Journeys by Heart: A Christology of Erotic Power* (New York: Crossroad, 1988); and Mary Grey, *Redeeming the Dream: Feminism, Redemption and Christian Tradition* (London: SPCK, 1989).
35 Maitland, 'Passionate prayer', p. 127.
36 Elizabeth Robertson, 'The corporeality of female sanctity in "The Life of Saint Margaret"' in Renate Blumenfeld-Kosinski and Timea Szell (eds), *Images of Sainthood in Medieval Europe* (Ithaca: Cornell University Press, 1991), pp. 268–81.
37 Maitland, 'Passionate prayer', p. 128.
38 Joanne Carlson Brown and Rebecca Parker, 'For God so loved the world' in Joanne Carlson Brown and Carole R. Bohn (eds), *Christianity, Patriarchy and Abuse* (Cleveland: The Pilgrim Press, 1989), p. 2.
39 Alison Webster, *Found Wanting: Women, Christianity and Sexuality* (London: Cassell, 1985), p. 89.
40 Gillian Cloke, *This Female Man of God: Women and Spiritual Power in the Patristic Age, AD 350–450* (London: Routledge, 1995), p. 213.
41 Woodward, *Making Saints*, p. 369.
42 The classic account of the history of canonization is Eric Waldron Kemp, *Canonisation and Authority in the Western Church* (Oxford: Oxford University Press, 1948).
43 John Mecklin, *The Passing of the Saint* (Chicago: University of Chicago Press, 1941).

44 Patrick Geary, 'Humiliation of the Saints' in Wilson, *Saints and Their Cults*, p. 133.
45 Weinstein and Bell, *Saints and Society*, p. 179.
46 Katherine and Charles H. George, 'Roman Catholic sainthood and social status: a statistical and analytical study', *Journal of Religion*, vol. 35, no. 2 (April 1955), pp. 85–98.
47 Weinstein and Bell, *Saints and Society*, pp. 220–37.
48 Woodward, *Making Saints*, p. 117.
49 Lawrence Cunningham, *The Meaning of Saints* (San Francisco: Harper and Row, 1980), p. 50.
50 *De Servorum Dei Beatificatione et Beatorum Canonizatione*, 4 vols (1734–38).
51 These positions had existed for at least two hundred years before Lambertini's reforms.
52 Similar misgivings have been expressed about the canonization of Fr Maximilian Kolbe who also died in Auschwitz in the year before Stein. Kolbe was founder of the Knights of the Immaculata, a missionary organization. He was imprisoned because of this and was canonized for taking the place of another prisoner in the starvation bunker. The singling out for sanctity of a handful of Catholics when six million Jews perished in the Holocaust is particularly galling to the many who believe that the Vatican could have done much more for the Jews than it did.
53 *Calendarium Romanum* (1969).
54 Michael Perham, *The Communion of Saints: An Examination of the Place of the Christian Dead in the Belief, Worship, and Calendars of the Church* (London: Alcuin Club/SPCK, 1980), pp. 147–8.
55 Woodward, *Making Saints*, p. 111.
56 Cited in Woodward, *Making Saints*, p. 35.
57 Topping, *Holy Mothers of Orthodoxy*.
58 See Carter Heyward, *Touching Our Strength: The Erotic as Power and the Love of God* (San Francisco: Harper and Row, 1989); Brock, *Journeys by Heart*; and my *Just Good Friends: Towards a Lesbian and Gay Theology of Relationships* (London: Mowbray, 1995).
59 Schüssler Fiorenza, *Discipleship of Equals*, p. 228.
60 Brock, *Journeys by Heart*, p. 51.
61 *The Passion of Saint Perpetua and Saint Felicity*, XII.
62 Heffernan, *Sacred Biography*, p. 283.
63 Heyward, *Touching Our Strength*, p. 11.
64 Carter Heyward, *Speaking of Christ: A Lesbian Feminist Voice* (New York: The Pilgrim Press, 1989).
65 Heyward, *Speaking of Christ*, p. 62.
66 Richard Kieckhefer and George D. Bond, *Sainthood: Its Manifestation in World Religions* (Berkeley: University of California Press, 1988), p. xiii.
67 Jane Stevenson, 'Early Irish saints: some uses of hagiography' in Clyde

Binfield (ed.), *Sainthood Revisioned: Studies in Hagiography and Biography* (Sheffield: Sheffield Academic Press, 1995), p. 26.

68 Rosemary Radford Ruether, 'Ecofeminism and healing ourselves, healing the earth', *Feminist Theology*, vol. 9 (May 1995), p. 61.

69 Daphne Hampson, *Theology and Feminism* (Basil Blackwell: Oxford, 1990), p. 140.

70 Hampson, *Theology and Feminism*, p. 142.

71 Ruether, 'Ecofeminism and healing ourselves, healing the earth', p. 52.

72 Schüssler Fiorenza, *Discipleship of Equals*, pp. 40–1.

73 Margaret Miles, 'Introduction' in Atkinson, Buchanan and Miles, *Immaculate and Powerful*, p. 2.

2

Patching the quilt: feminist readings of saints

Patching theology

Perhaps a more palatable metaphor for the feminist reconstruction of Christian history and Christian doctrine is that of the patchwork – a metaphor used by Margaret Miles, who points out that whereas men believe that they create culture out of nothing, women have been presented with a 'cultural fabric' usually not of their own making, though it may concern them. They have had to sift through the fabric, identifying which pieces enhance and which pieces harm their lives: 'Women have selected and arranged in new configurations pieces of the cultural tapestry and in so doing have created strong and unique new patterns, patterns that display the vivid colours of their experience.'[1] The patchwork quilt may be a particularly appropriate metaphor in this context. I think of three uses of the quilt. First, to commemorate the Ecumenical Decade of Churches in Solidarity with Women, the so-called Durham quilt was made by various European women's groups. Each group produced a panel in which they commemorated a notable woman from the past or the present. These panels were then sewn together and the quilt unveiled at a special service in Durham Cathedral in 1992. I have on my desk a large postcard on which twelve of the panels are reproduced. The panels commemorate: Sue Ryder, Mary Burdon, Hildegard of Bingen, Penny Jamieson, Hannah Marshman, Kate Tristram, Dorothee Sölle, Mary Ward, Rose Macaulay, Mary Sumner, St Catherine of Siena and Eva Burrows. The Durham quilt testifies to the importance of past women to women struggling today; it testifies to the importance of women saints in that struggle. It also demonstrates women's willingness to look beyond the male canon of saints to seek out and make visible other women who did not make it into the 'official' list. And finally it testifies to the women's sense of a

[49]

direct line of continuity between someone like St Catherine of Siena
and Penny Jamieson, one of the first female bishops in the Anglican
Communion. There are some qualities, some experiences, that can
bind them together in the same quilt.

The second type of quilt that comes to mind is the friendship quilt.
This type of quilt was very popular in North America in the middle
of the nineteenth century. These quilts were made as gifts for friends,
sisters and other relations. They were made by women, usually for
women. They were personalized, with details about the maker and
receiver written or stitched into the design, perhaps with additional
advice or poems added. Mary Hunt draws out two important
points about the quilts: first, even though each one was individual
it is remarkable how much alike they are, and second, these quilts
are often the only evidence that has survived for the existence of the
women who made and received them. Linda Otto Lipsett has
observed: 'It was not woman's desire, however, to be forgotten. And
in one simple, unpretentious way, she created a medium that would
outlive even many of her husband's houses, barns and fences: she
signed her name in friendship onto cloth and, in her own way, cried
out, "Remember me." '[2] Women entrusted their memories to their
friends and to the power of friendship, and the large number of quilts
that have survived testifies to the wisdom of their trust. Hunt uses
the friendship quilt as a metaphor for feminist theology. Just as
quilts, though unique, share common characteristics, so with women
and their spiritual tapestries. No one will take women's spiritual
experience seriously except women, so it is essential that we write
ourselves into theology, and the best way to do that is through
communal work. We have to preserve not only our own theologizing
but also the theology of the women who have gone before us:
'Through little help from the theological establishment, which to date
still pays them scant attention, the work of earlier women is known.
. . . Still I shudder to think how much has been lost, the tattered quilts
of our collective history turned into dust rags. It cannot happen
again.'[3]

The third quilt that comes to my mind and will be familiar to
anyone in the lesbian and gay community is the AIDS quilt. All over
the world partners, friends, family of those who have died of an
AIDS-related illness commemorate the unique life of that person in
a cloth panel which is attached to others and forms a massive quilt
usually unveiled in a public place on World AIDS Day. Some people
living with AIDS choose to make their own panel representing their

life and character as they would wish to be remembered. Once again people who would otherwise be written out of history except as a carrier, 'innocent' or 'guilty', as the dominant culture constructs it, of 'the' disease of the late twentieth century, write themselves into history through friendship and solidarity. Those who make their own panel often do so to ensure that they are remembered by their friends for their life and not for their death. Carter Heyward offers the following reflections upon the AIDS quilt:

> Closure, termination, and death can be cruel and harsh, unjust and unwelcome. In friendship, however, the end is not final. Friends bear each other up here and now and well into eternity, the realm outside of time as we measure it. This bearing up of one another, the capacity for undying friendship, is our passion: it is what we suffer and celebrate together; it is what we are willing to die for, hence what we are able to live for. It secures our love-making as well as our leave-taking in faith that our story is not over. The AIDS quilt is a powerful sign of this passion and faith.[4]

I am going to suggest that in these reflections upon what we might call 'the theology of quilts' lie the seeds for a regenerated, refashioned theology of sainthood. But before diving into that task, and as a preliminary to it, it is necessary to spell out in more detail why the theology of sainthood is a worthwhile focus for feminist theologizing.

Rending rhetoric asunder

In the previous chapter I presented a deliberately negative view of female saints and the concept of sainthood, based upon a feminist analysis of the lives of the saints and the development of a doctrine of sainthood as they were fashioned and handed down to us by men. But from its earliest days feminist theology has recognized that the texts of Church history as they have been handed down to us are not, as we have been led to believe, 'fact' or 'truth', but what Elisabeth Schüssler Fiorenza has called rhetoric, i.e. written in the middle of struggles by people who took sides in that struggle. Fiorenza has noted that the feminist task, when presented with this rhetoric, is to deconstruct it and reconstruct it from the perspective of those whom it condemns or silences. Women's experience teaches them that there have always been women who have been active in the world, although their achievements have not been recorded. Their activity may lie behind the history that has been recorded and it is possible to detect their presence through the contradictions or fractures in the texts. In the case of the saints, we do not usually have to look for shadows between words – here are women at the centre of narratives, whose lives are recorded, often in great detail. Certainly those lives have been shaped, manipulated by the male-Church as part of a theological rhetoric, yet a superficial reading of the lives of women saints demonstrates that rhetoric cannot contain them. They burst out of the corsets made by priests, bishops and Popes and from across sometimes hundreds of years they call out to us, asking us to look closer and to feel the solidarity of common struggle.

To give but a taste of the way that the bonds are broken, no gloss can hide the fact that, according to the *Commentary on Broccán's Hymn*, the ancient Irish saint Brigit of Kildare was ordained as a bishop by Bishop Mel. Some of the authors of the lives of St Brigit were rather embarrassed by the story but none tried to deny it, although some attributed the action to the bishop's overzealousness. Indeed, the lives of St Brigit reveal a woman who exercised considerable power in the Church and society of her day, to whom men and women flocked for spiritual guidance and to whom even representatives of Rome came, rather than expecting her to go to them as was usual.[5] St Hilda of Whitby, a woman of royal blood, only turned to religious life in her middle years but proceeded to found a community in Northumbria, become abbess of a community at Hartlepool and in 657 found the double monastery at Whitby, which under her leadership became famous for being run according to strict principles of equality, for its education of the clergy (at least five of whom were subsequently made bishops), and for the production of illustrated manuscripts and works on mathematics. It was also known as a great centre of hospitality. In particular Hilda became patron of the Anglo-Saxon cowherd Caedmon who was the first native English poet. Hilda's considerable influence is best illustrated by her ability to persuade King Oswy to convene a synod at Whitby to deal with the tensions between Romanizing Christians and those who adhered to Celtic Christianity and the Irish rite. Hilda herself supported the Irish rite, but the rhetoric of Bishop Wilfrid who was pro-Roman won the day and Hilda accepted the consensus opinion. Although her biographer, Bede, was anxious to portray Hilda as a woman dependent upon men for her education and a loyal daughter of the Church, the woman who presses her face against the window pane of the narrative is a woman of considerable strength and influence who exercised leadership in a manner that will always be profoundly shocking to those who have swallowed the rhetoric of male-Church as historical truth. A similar story can found in the life of St Pulcheria, an empress of Byzantium who always lived the life of a nun. She was responsible for convening the Council of Chalcedon in 451 which was a milestone in the development of 'orthodox' christology. She was hailed as the 'light of orthodoxy' and the 'Protectress of the Faith' and was able to convince bishops to adopt her own ecclesiastical policies with little difficulty. The respect and influence she enjoyed is well illustrated by the fact that on Easter Sundays she was permitted to accompany the Patriarch and the emperor into the sanctuary of the Megale Ekklesia and take communion there.

Feminist scholars have shown particular interest in the figure of Mary Magdalen and the way she is portrayed in the Gospels that did not make it into the canon of Scripture. (The formation of the canon was also undertaken in the midst of and in response to struggles within the Church; feminists therefore operate a hermeneutic of suspicion when dealing with the scriptural canon as they do when dealing with all aspects of male-Church.) In most of the non-canonical Gospels that we possess, Mary is portrayed neither as a repentant sinner nor as a prostitute. On the contrary, these Gospels choose to emphasize her role (certainly hinted at in the canonical Gospels but largely ignored in lives and portraits of her from then on) as a leading disciple, 'an apostle to the apostles' and close companion of Christ. In the *Gospel of Philip* she is portrayed almost as the incarnation of Sophia (wisdom). In the *Gospel of Mary* there is some explicit tension (again implicit in the canonical Gospels) between her and St Peter after the resurrection, but it is Mary and not Peter who takes charge of the disciples. The *beata peccatrix* (blessed sinner) and *castissima meretrix* (most chaste prostitute) figure that made her the most famous and one of the best loved saints of the Middle Ages is nowhere to be seen.[6]

Karen Scott has shown how Raymond of Capua's life of Catherine of Siena moulded her into the pattern of late medieval piety, obscuring the fact that Catherine herself (as her own writings testify) understood herself as an apostle. She felt called not to fit into pre-existing ecclesiastical categories of female roles but to be an itinerant preacher, peacemaker, reformer and apostle. Mary Magdalen was an inspiration to her and the only legitimation she sought was her calling from God. Catherine waded into the heart of papal politics and church reform, as well as pastoral work, whilst recognizing that

her calling was not shared or meant to be by all. She had the authority to persuade the Pope to walk barefoot through the streets of Rome
as a form of penance. She was also a universalist. Whilst sometimes
reflecting the socio-religious and cultural construction of women of
her age, she did not apply this to herself: 'We have been put [here]
to sow the word of God and to reap the fruit of salvation . . .
Everyone must be solicitous in his own trade . . . and not bury the
talent.'[7]

St Thérèse of Lisieux is a perfect example of the modern female
saint being portrayed visually and textually in terms that obscure
something of her real personality. Thomas Merton's first impressions
of her were that she was 'a pious doll in the imagination of a lot of
sentimental old women'.[8] The text of the 'Little Flower' is capable of
being read another way in which she emerges as the tall, strong tree,
for, like Catherine, Thérèse was motivated primarily not by a desire
to conform to already existing patterns of spirituality but by her own
distinctive and original theological vision, the essence of which was
a spiritual liberty at odds with contemporary notions of spiritual
direction and developments.[9] Also against the conventions of the
time, she was clear that all Christians were equal and the path to
holiness was open to all because it was based not upon impossible
demands but simply upon love. 'Ironically, though Thérèse's canonization process was designed – like all canonizations – to prove she
practiced "heroic virtue", Thérèse rejected that ideal of holiness: the
extraordinary; what others could observe and testify about.'[10] Conn
challenges the popular notion, inspired by the literature produced
to aid her canonization, that (in the words of Kelly and Rogers'
caricature):

> Forbidden because of her fragility to starve, whip, or mutilate herself
> as the Great Virgin-Martyr-Saints of the past had done, Theresa
> discovered that she could make herself beatifically miserable by
> enduring the *little* things. She would not brush away a fly, or scratch
> an itch. She would sleep under a heavy blanket in the summer heat,
> and without it in winter. She would piously and smilingly endure the
> irritating faults of others (while keeping careful count).[11]

Conn believes that most commentators have missed the irony in
many of Thérèse's accounts of these events. Her 'little way' was not
so much about enduring the niggling annoyances with heroic virtue,
but eschewing heroic virtue altogether and finding God in the
ordinary and everyday, a very feminist notion and presumably why

she became patron of the worker-priest movement. She did not see herself or anyone else climbing a ladder to perfection but taking an elevator straight to God, an elevator which she identified with a divine maternal embrace.[12] All the lives of Thérèse record the fact she had to wrestle with obstructive clerics in order to enter Carmel, directly appealing to the Pope himself, breaking all conventions during an audience. Very few record the fact that towards the end of her life she confided to a sister that she felt a vocation to be a priest, regarding it as a grace that God was ending her life at the time when she would have been ordained if she had been a man. Nor did she demonstrate much 'ladylike' modesty when she declared that she was born for glory and destined to be a great saint. There is much about Thérèse which feminists still might find cloying and indigestible but it is possible to offer a feminist rhetorical reading of her life, in which even the 'Little Flower' bursts from her metaphorical saintly corsets. Nowhere is this clearer perhaps than in visual representations of Thérèse. In pious iconography a child's face with dark shadows under the eyes stares seriously whilst she clutches a bunch of roses and a crucifix. But Thérèse also left behind remarkably different photographs of herself. She is larger, and humour and mischief run across her face; she looks very happy and human. Among her favourite saints were Teresa of Avila and Joan of Arc, neither of whom exactly fitted the patterns of female piety in their own day or beyond! When even St Thérèse of Lisieux has a forceful character that belies the delicate 'Little Flower' image carefully crafted by a Church hierarchy facing the initial challenges of modern feminism, then any and every female saint, however apparently antithetical to feminism, deserves a second look.

In 1975 Pope Paul VI canonized the woman who was to become the first saint of the United States of America. In many respects the life of Elizabeth Seton (1774–1821), as it was fashioned after her death for the purposes of canonization by a Jesuit, fits the mould of a standard female saint.[13] Born into a good Episcopalian family, Elizabeth Bailey married William Magee Seton, a businessman of considerable wealth. They had five children and a decade of happiness together before all started to go wrong. Her husband was made bankrupt and became terminally ill, dying in quarantine in Italy where they had gone to aid his health. Within a year Elizabeth Seton had converted to Catholicism, which resulted in alienation from her family and consequent poverty, and proceeded to found Catholic schools and become a religious. Her sanctity was thought to reside in her acceptance of all kinds of hardship and loss – she lost two of her daughters to tuberculosis (the same disease that killed their father and was eventually to take their mother) – whilst always looking beyond her own suffering to the needs of others. She is therefore presented in popular piety as the archetypal mother, cheerfully enduring every pain and offering it all up, unquestioningly, to God. But yet again a fainter but distinct voice calls from the text, the voice of a woman who felt confident enough in her own spiritual integrity and authority to respond to her husband's request for the last rites by devising a liturgy herself; a woman who managed to pursue her dream and vocation of entering the religious life, founding a new order (the Daughters of St Joseph) whilst continuing to mother her children – thus overcoming the dualistic division between the religious life and family life so entrenched in the Catholic tradition and mentality. Contrary to popular piety, she was deeply affected by death and other tragedy and all her life was deeply frustrated by the values and consequent behaviour demonstrated by the social circle in which her family moved. This different side to Seton is revealed in the letters she wrote to a childhood friend, Julianna Scott, a correspondence which continued for most of her life. Like any woman who founded a new religious order or wanted to pursue a spiritual path which diverged from the contemporary conventions of spiritual life, Seton required great strength and assertiveness as she had to wrestle with opposition and obstruction.

This is clearly the case with one of the two female doctors of the Church, Teresa of Avila. Mary Collins comments: 'The Church which canonised her and which named her doctor nevertheless represses the memory of the conflictive process by which an independent Church woman set out her teaching and prevailed. Why? For what purpose? And whose?'[14] Well, certainly not women's. This gregarious, highly intelligent, impulsive and impatient woman, whom a contemporary described as large and laughing, was put into a convent by her father after a rather hazy incident which she described as mortal sin and in terms of being blinded by passion, and which involved a female cousin. It is highly probable that she became romantically involved with this woman.[15] She did not remain in this Augustinian community, although she enjoyed the life and the friendships she made there. She was clear, however, that she did not want to be married and eventually entered the Carmel of the Incarnation, possibly attracted by the Carmelites' claim to Jewish roots, for her family were of Jewish origin. She defied her father's wishes by entering. The life of a nun in the Incarnation was extremely comfortable and whilst the Reformation raged throughout northern Europe Teresa and her fellow sisters were enjoying a free and almost extravagant existence. However, Teresa became increasingly unhappy with the tension between that way of life and the original Carmelite vision. With the encouragement and co-operation of several of her fellow nuns she set out, at the age of 40, to establish a second Carmelite convent in Avila, with no financial endowments and based upon the original Carmelite rule. The plan met with considerable opposition from the order and from the civil authorities but Teresa pressed ahead. Her personal convictions were now reinforced by visions which she was always rather embarrassed about and kept largely to herself and to her confessor. However, these visions gave her the confidence to challenge and if necessary defy ecclesiastics. Collins notes that she was always careful to have the confidence of several theologians, religious superiors and confessors at once, in order that at least one would legitimate her convictions. In other words, she knew how to play the system. One confessor noted wearily that he would rather argue with all the theologians in creation that with 'that woman'.[16] She herself had a rather low opinion of most of her confessors, who, she felt, did not understand women and who also lacked intellectual sophistication. The exception to this was her extraordinary friendship with Fray Jeronimo Gracián. They met when he was 30 and she 60 and their friendship lasted seven years until her death. At first she saw this young, dynamic and learned Carmelite who was filled with zeal for reform as a very useful ally. Then he became her confessor and a passionately intense relationship developed between them. Only her letters to him survive so it is impossible to get the full story. But she relates a vision which deeply troubled her in which God married her to her confessor; she also felt his sufferings in her body and worried about him a great deal. But in the end this 'marriage well arranged', as she put it, hit the rocks somewhat.[17] This passionate attachment to people was an important part of Teresa's personality and not, for her, in any way incompatible with the religious life. 'I have no defence against affection', she once remarked, and her love of people and of food is amply attested to – a greater contrast with Rose of Lima (who was born shortly after Teresa's death) could not be imagined. 'My dear, you must know there is a time for partridges and a time for penance', she is said to have remarked to a maid obviously amazed by her enthusiastic consumption of the bird. She also admitted that she could be bribed with a sardine. She taught her nuns to dance with joy on feast days. Again here we have a woman before whom dualisms dissolve, a religious concerned to return to the original vision of her order but who still loved her body, her food and other people and who saw no contradiction in this. She was a woman who loved her own flesh. It is for this reason that Teresa's experience of Christ as lover and spouse is far less sado-masochistic than some women's. In her description of the process of union with the divine lover in *The Interior Castle* the focus is on the gradual removal of sufferings as the soul becomes more confident in the love of God, and the human and divine bound towards one another in passionate love and unity. And although, like Catherine of Siena, she echoed standard contemporary views of women's lack of intellectual ability, she evidently did not apply them to herself.

In 1560 she finally received papal approval for her project and for the next twenty years she devoted herself to founding communities, fifteen in all. A contemporary reported that, despite being the foundress of these communities, 'she did not wish to exercise any authority in any houses she happened to be in. On the contrary she would serve in the refectory, cook in the kitchen . . . She was fond of taking advice and would take it from the youngest in the house.'[18] This desire to base her communities on friendship and mutuality rather than on authoritarian hierarchy eventually paid off. For opposition to her work did not cease with papal approval. Suspicion of mystics was rife at this time, when acknowledgement of any kind of authority other than papal authority was regarded as dangerous and heretical. Teresa became the object of the Inquisition's interest and, although she was never charged with anything, she was ordered to write her life.

When, under her influence, St John of the Cross reformed the Carmelite communities of men, many in her order felt threatened by her power and she was ordered to take over an unreformed community for three years. When her communities were threatened with dissolution, she appealed directly to King Philip II, persuading him to make Gracián superior of all discalced Carmelites in Spain. But perhaps the ultimate triumph came when an opponent of Teresa, who was presiding over the election of a prioress at the Incarnation, forbade the nuns to vote for Teresa. Fifty-five out of the 99 nuns disobeyed. Teresa described the scene:

> As each of them gave him her vote, he excommunicated and anathe-
> matised her, ground the voting papers with his fist, struck them

repeatedly and finally burnt them. These religious have been excommunicated for the last fortnight. He has forbidden them to hear Mass, and no one, not even their confessors or relations, is allowed to speak to them. The wonderful part of it is that the day after this election of thumps, the Father Provincial sent for the nuns who had voted for me and told them to make their election. They replied that there was no election to make, for they had made it. Whereupon he again excommunicated them.[19]

Here we have a case of women supporting each other against what for them were the direst threats possible, and defying the frightening power of male authority for the sake of justice for themselves. This was a profoundly subversive act and the frustration shown by the clergy towards these nuns was mirrored in many encounters with Teresa throughout her life. As well as being a reformer Teresa was also a theologian. She interpreted her visions and produced a highly sophisticated theology of the soul in her *Interior Castle* which later was to earn her the title of 'Doctor of the Church', although the Vatican's recognition of her greatness may have had more to do with the fact that it wished to build an image of itself as appreciating the importance of women in the Church whilst at the same time explicitly excluding them from ordained ministry. Teresa's own prayer 'From sour-faced saints, good Lord deliver us' was answered in her own person and in the lives of every other founder or reformer who took on the ecclesiastical establishment trusting in her own theology.

Mary Collins has suggested that a feminist eye should be cast over a modern founder of a religious order and someone regarded as a living saint – Mother Teresa of Calcutta. Christopher Hitchens' rhetorical reading of Mother Teresa's life for his television programme produced a 'Hell's Angel', yet feminists would want to operate a hermeneutic of suspicion with even this subversive reading, because what Hitchens did not draw attention to was the fact that 'Mother Teresa of Calcutta too prevailed in her own vocation because she refused to be deterred by established institutions and approved behaviours'.[20] She left the religious order she had entered in the 1940s in order to follow what she believed to be a divine call which no ecclesiastical obstacle could prevent her following. Perhaps it was her very strength and independence that led churchmen to adopt her so quickly when she became Mother Teresa of Calcutta; maybe they sought to neutralize her potential power before she could use it in ways that would embarrass them.

One saint who most obviously and famously breaks apart the bonds of rhetoric is Joan of Arc. Joan is perhaps the best documented woman of the Middle Ages, the prime source of information about her being the record of her trial for heresy which took place between 9 January and 30 May 1431. As Marina Warner has noted, Joan is a universal figure but fits none of the feminine types:

> neither a queen, nor a courtesan, nor a beauty, nor a mother, nor an artist of one kind or another, nor – until the extremely recent date of 1920 when she was canonised – a saint. She eludes the categories in which women have normally achieved a higher status that gives them immortality, and yet she gained it.[21]

She gained it by breaking almost every patriarchal rule in the book. She was a peasant girl who became a national leader, a woman who took on 'male' roles and 'male' clothes. She trusted in the authority of her 'voices' rather than in the authority of the Church, she was a woman who mixed freely with men and yet was not a 'loose woman' (her virginity was attested to at the trial) and finally she was a convicted heretic who was subsequently declared a saint. Joan was the incarnation of inversion, she disrupted notions of what was 'natural' which were so precious at the time, as men sought to gain control of their environment, imaging it often as a wild enemy to be conquered. Her sporting of 'male' attire (soldier's uniform) particularly worried her inquisitors and was the subject of no less than five charges brought against her. Female transvestism was about social inversion: by dressing as men women are perceived to be challenging male status, for in most societies influenced by Christianity male and female belong to different social stratifications, the woman below the man – and indeed the building blocks of society are built upon these foundations. In such a clearly stratified society, male looks and roles and behaviours have to be very clearly defined, as do women's, to keep that society functioning. When a woman looks and behaves 'like a man' she destabilizes the pillars of patriarchal society for she demonstrates that the principles on which it is based are false. It is interesting that a poem written on transvestism around the same time that Joan lived describes the practice as 'idolatry'.[22] To undermine the patriarchal stratification of society is to cease to worship the true God who orders and legitimates the stratifications, and one can understand why Joan was labelled a witch. Much speculation has since taken place as to why she wore these clothes even when not fighting. Some suggest that it was to avoid rape in prison. Joan herself would never explain the decision except to say that it was what her voices commanded. She resumed 'female' clothing only once, when she abjured on 14 May. She may have been tricked into signing a recantation but in any case was sentenced to life in solitary confinement. Four days later, after some stern talk from her voices, she had resumed her old dress. She may not have liked her costume much but to her it was intricately connected with her ministry and she would not give it up even when tempted with what she longed for most – Mass and communion.[23]

There is a long tradition in Christian hagiography of female transvestism – women having to assume the garb of men in order to achieve what they believed they were called to be – although, unlike Joan, most pretended to be men. Most, like Joan, had had to flee their parents to avoid marriage. Like Teresa, Joan trusted absolutely in the authority of her own 'voices', whom she identified as St Michael, St Margaret of Antioch and St Katherine of Alexandria, and who first came to her when she was thirteen. This gave her an outspoken assertiveness which made a defending lawyer unnecessary and was bound to antagonize her judges. To give but some examples:

INTERROGATOR: When you saw your Voices was any special light visible?
JOAN: Light shines on others besides you.

INTERROGATOR: Did St Michael appear to you naked?
JOAN: Think you that my master had not the wherewith to clothe him?

INTERROGATOR: Do you submit to the judgement of the Church?
JOAN: I submit to Our Lord, who sent me on my mission; to our Lady, to all the blessed saints and the holy ones of paradise.

INTERROGATOR: Then you do not submit to the Church?
JOAN: As I see it, Our Lord and His Church are one, so there will be no difficulty there.

INTERROGATOR: Would you feel bound to reveal the whole truth to the Pope?
JOAN: I demand to be taken to him and I will give my answer before him.[24]

And when she was threatened with instruments of torture she once again demonstrated that the authority of her voices overruled all human ones:

Truly, should you tear me limb from limb and cause my soul to leave its body, I would tell you nothing but what I have already told. I have asked audience from my Voices as to whether I should submit to the Church, and they have said to me: 'If you wish your Master to come to your aid, you must leave the judgement of your actions to Him.' I also asked my Voices if I would be burned, and in reply they told me: 'Leave that in God's hands. He will help you.'[25]

Her authority was also of course confirmed by popular belief in her divine mission. In the fifteenth century numerous prophecies swept through France predicting the coming of a virgin saviour. The visionary Marie d'Avignon had predicted that an armed woman would save the kingdom, others such as Christine de Pisan (a contemporary of Joan's who took a particular interest in celebrating the lives of strong women) were convinced that Merlin, the Sibyl and the Venerable Bede had all foreseen her coming.[26] Whether Joan knew of these predictions or not, her only sense of authority came from her voices. Everybody of course believed that God cared about and was involved in contemporary history and that, indeed, God took sides. Joan believed this with a passion, a passion that lifted her above all social and ecclesiastical convention. When asked by an interrogator (representing the English cause) why St Margaret did not speak to Joan in English, Joan's reply would have been that of most French people: 'Why should she speak English, since she does not support the English cause?' What is extraordinary about this reply is that it was made by a woman in direct defiance of ecclesiastical authority. She was a country woman who became intimately involved in politics, who became empowered to lead and to change things. Warner has pointed out that the village from which Joan hailed, Domrémy, was divided between two secular and ecclesiastical lords, one part belonging to France, one to the Holy Roman Empire, with inevitable tensions which had profoundly affected Joan. 'She had a natural inclination for clear-cut situations, with identifiable centres of authority . . . She liked unity, organisation, rallied groups.'[27] Warner believes this was also why she liked bells and heard her voices when the church bells were rung, because in medieval villages bells unified the community, calling them together for worship, for communal displays of feasting and mourning, and warning them of impending danger: 'A bell peals for cohesiveness, not chaos, for harmony, not division.'[28] All her life she was the victim of split loyalties and she finally gave her life to the situation she detested most – the necessity of choosing between the Church and her own voices. Joan's mission therefore arose out of her own experience, it was rooted in her experience of the world and it was into that experience that the divine pealed like a bell. She died, burnt at the stake, wearing a paper mitre (another 'male' garment) bearing the words 'Heretic, Relapsed Sinner, Apostate, Idolater'. Joan's mother Isabelle Romée played a large part in securing her daughter's rehabilitation and by 1455 had succeeded. No one should doubt that it was political expediency that led the Church to denounce its own trial, just as it was political expediency, fear of communism and a desire to encourage movements against communism that led to her canonization in 1920. She was not declared a martyr – the Church does not so honour people it has itself killed – but a virgin.

Perhaps no saint has struck such a chord with feminists, secular and religious, as Joan. In particular, feminists have picked up on parts of Joan's story which link her with the women-affirming so-called 'old religion' of pre-Christian Europe which blended in so well with imported Christianity until that Christianity was forcibly Romanized. Certainly, much effort was made at her trial to associate Joan with witchcraft. Reference was made to a beech tree in Domrémy, where in the middle of Lent villagers gathered to hang garlands of flowers and to make votive offerings as well as to sing and to dance. It stood near a healing spring and in the middle of an oak wood. L'Arbre des Fées or L'Arbre des Dames was also supposed to be the home of fairies. Joan denied that she heard her voices under the tree but it was a widely held belief that she did, possibly because it was prophesied that a saviour would come from an oak wood. To the children and their parents who took part in the annual ceremony the practice was undoubtedly nothing unusual, but to her interrogators it stank of witchcraft and Druidism. In a famous and extremely controversial study of witchcraft Margaret Murray suggested that Joan was a member of a secret coven.[29] Certainly there is something about the manner in which Joan came to be perceived that reached beyond the bounds of a strictly Christian tradition. It is highly unlikely that she knew herself as Joan *of Arc* or d'Arc (though her family name may have been Darc).[30] Her name was refashioned into d'Arc in the sixteenth century when there was a conscious attempt to portray Joan as an Amazon. Tales of the ferocious female tribe with their deadly bow-and-arrow skills were around in Joan's day, and some have suggested that Joan assumed the ancient role of the Warrior Maiden which was deeply engraved in the pre-Christian psyche of the Celtic peoples; and that in that role she offered herself as a scapegoat, a substitute sacrifice for the Dauphin, who represented the 'horned-god of the people' who had dominated Celtic society. Certainly Joan became the object of popular devotion and was believed to have miraculous powers.[31] She was accused of allowing people to treat her as a living saint, but she was evidently deeply uncomfortable with other people's devotion to her, refusing to 'perform' the miracles or fortune-telling they sought from her. Whether it is true that people flocked to her because they recognized in this warrior maiden some echo of a ceremonial figure from pre-Christian times, a fifteenth-century Boudicca, is a matter of interpretation.[32] What is clear is that Joan did not fit into any category of female piety available to her through the Church. She was essentially a prophet and, therefore, like almost every prophet in Christian history came under suspicion of heresy, but she was also a warrior prophet and contemporaries had to look back to the Bible – to Judith and Deborah – to find examples of such women.

A feminist reading of the life of Joan is not a merely twentieth-century phenomenon. Marina Warner points out that the issues of what we now call feminism were as alive in the fifteenth century as they are in our own, although the debate was largely confined to an educated élite. Warner draws attention to the part that the figure of Joan of Arc played in the debates. Christine de Pisan used Joan's example to flout the misogyny of Jean de Meung, who completed *Le Roman de la Rose*, and thereafter she became a central figure in an ongoing debate about the intelligence, leadership ability and virtues of women.[33] Joan is one of the few female figures in Christian history whose life has always been subjected to a pro-women reading. She has always had a particular resonance with those other women who have also been accused of subverting nature and seeking to overturn Christianity – lesbians.[34] In Joan's case it is not just that she bursts from her corsets, it is that no one could get her into the corsets in the first place. In many ways she represents all that men with institutional power in the Christian tradition have always feared about women – uncontrollable power – and that was why she was martyred, but her spirit could not so easily be disposed of. As Kelly and Rogers end their account of her life: 'We invite anyone who has a word to say against her to step outside and say it.'[35]

This brief look at alternative readings of the lives of some women saints at least begins to suggest why the saints are worth rediscovering or sticking with. Even the saints that popular piety or Vatican politics present as specific antidotes to feminism are capable of a feminist reading. In other words it is possible to feel a solidarity with women who have lived and striven and struggled within the same Christian community. They can therefore be part of the sacred and subversive memory of women-Church. It is essential for women to root ourselves in solidarity with the past, to re-member our dismembered history in order to patch together our quilts, because, as I have argued elsewhere, it is only when we weave together our own personal experience with that of others, including that of our ancestors in faith and struggle, that we begin to get any sense of the movement of the divine in history.[36] Only when we have patched together our pieces of treasure from the rubbish bin does a pattern begin to emerge, a pattern which can point us in the right direction. Israel Baal Shem Tov, the Hasidic sage, believed that 'to forget is to prolong the exile; to remember is the beginning of redemption'. In offering a feminist rhetorical reading of the lives of the female saints, women seek to redeem the past, to buy it back from male interpreters in order to claim a central space in their world. Milan Kundera writes: 'The struggle of people against power is the struggle of memory against forgetting.'[37]

The women with whose lives we are concerned struggled against the powers of forgetting and largely won. In Joan's case it is clear that women played a central role in keeping her memory as a subversive woman alive and it is highly probable that the same is true in other cases. This leads us to the other dimension of sainthood that should make feminists and all other Christians involved in liberation movements think before dismissing it – it is clearly a doctrine and practice that arose 'from below' rather than being imposed from above. Even though bishops moved quickly to take control of the practice of canonization, and even though it became a political tool in the hands of the hierarchy, proof of 'popular' devotion has always been an essential component in the proof of sanctity. When the hierarchy approves of the cult of a saint, it may seek to manipulate the representation of the saint or use her or him for its own purposes, but by and large it was not the prime mover in stirring up popular devotion. In terms of the feminist theology of revelation developed by Mary Grey, with the saints we are clearly dealing with a Sophia model of revelation rather than a Logos one. The Logos model which has dominated in Christian history identifies revelation with truths revealed to and in some kind of authoritative source. It is a top-down model: revelation cascades from the divine, down the hierarchy and falls first, of course, into the laps of men who pass it down the chain until it eventually 'hits' women. This model serves to disguise the part played in the formation of doctrine by the patriarchal male agenda. The Sophia or Wisdom model is a bottom-up model of revelation: God is located not above but in the midst of creation. Revelation therefore emerges as a mist from the ground, from amongst the ordinary. Grey uses the Sophia or Wisdom myth to emphasize that revelation can and does occur in connectedness, in the connecting of people with each other, in their reconnection with their past and particularly with the forgotten voices of the past.[38] In the cult of the saints we have a clear example of a Sophia-based revelation; it may be subsequently adopted into a Logos model, but in its origins it is clearly an emerging rather than a cascading form of revelation. And the fact that feminist readings of the lives of the female saints, even after they have gone through the process of 'Logosifying', are possible, could be interpreted as indicating the continuing presence of Sophia in their stories, the Sophia from which they originally emerged. Granted, then, that it is possible to redeem female saints, is it possible to redeem the theology of sainthood?

Hints at redemption

Perhaps the most convincing reason why we should look at the concept of sainthood again from a feminist perspective is the part that women saints played in the lives of women saints and other Christian women. Sts Margaret and Katherine were the guiding forces (with St Michael) of Joan of Arc. Joan herself, along with Teresa of Avila, St Agnes and St Cecilia, was extremely important to Thérèse of Lisieux. Mary Magdalen had a particular appeal to Teresa of Avila. The saint whose feast day it was is often reported as appearing to medieval mystics. Hildegard of Bingen and Elizabeth of Schönau both shared a particular devotion to St Ursula. These women evidently found in the female saints of past ages some kind of positive endorsement that went beyond mere admiration and inspiration. So these women themselves, by their devotion to each other, challenge us to make some sense of the devotion for ourselves.

The most authoritative account of the development of the cult of the saints in Christianity has been written by Peter Brown.[39] Brown demolishes the Enlightenment notions that there was a distinction between 'popular' and 'intellectual' belief in the early Church, and that the cult of the saints reflects the vulgar beliefs of the uneducated masses. Often 'popular' belief which is dismissed and disparaged by scholars is particularly associated with women. People like Hume and

Gibbon assumed that 'popular' religion was only accessible as a concept to and capable of analysis by the intellectual élite and that it never changed, so that it is quite often asserted in writings upon the saints that they were simply Christianized versions of ancient deities and that the masses continued their devotion barely aware of a change of religion. Brown demonstrates that the cult of the saints actually belies this dualistic reading of Christian history: devotion to the saints was universal in early Christianity and indeed continued to be so. He also argues that the development of the Christian theology of sainthood represents a marked fissure with the theologies of the Roman Empire. The non-Christian peoples of the Roman Empire certainly venerated their dead, particularly their heroic dead, but there was no sense that these enjoyed particular intimacy with the divine, as came to be the belief in Christianity. For Brown what the Christian cult of the saints represented in the ancient world was radical and scandalous – a breaking down of some of the most precious metaphysical boundaries – between earth and heaven, divinity and humanity, the living and the dead. This defeating of dualisms must resonate with Christian feminists because it is an essential aspect of the feminist project to dismantle the mind-set that seeks to structure reality in terms of absolute opposites, with one superior to the other. Such dualism has always affected women negatively because they have always been identified with the wrong side of the equation: men/women; mind/body; reason/emotion; leaders/followers etc. So here we have our first rich pickings from the 'rubbish' heap of the theology of sainthood, the first piece of cloth from the ragbag of Christian tradition, something that might be redeemable from a feminist perspective.

Brown goes on to note that another barrier Christianity broke through in its dealings in general, but particularly manifest in its theology of sainthood, was the boundary of kinship groups.[40] Care for the dead, normally confined in Roman society to the family, was opened up to all: the dead belonged to everyone. The martyrs were not perceived as belonging to one family but as products of and belonging to (in life and in death) the whole Christian community, because at the heart of the gospel message was a subversion of traditional notions of family. The *basileia* of God was to be constructed not on the basis of the patriarchal family but on the basis of a new form of kinship which transcended all social boundaries.[41] All belonged to all and in the *ekklesia*, the new form of community that emerged, women and men, rich and poor, slave and free were now defined in terms of their common faith and vision. This is what made Christianity so profoundly socially subversive and led to the persecution that produced the martyrs who reflect that subversiveness: men and women, rich and poor, free and slaves. Brown indicates that the earliest interventions of bishops in the cult of the saints were actually to prevent the familializing of the cult of the saints, i.e. the buying up of the bodies of the martyrs by wealthy individuals or families and the restriction of access to the relics to blood-family members. He also records that Augustine sought to intervene to stop the practice of 'feasting' on martyrs' graves because it caused social division – wealthy families ate expensive and extravagant food and apparently did not share it with less well-off devotees.[42]

By that time Christianity had largely channelled its highly subversive vision of a community of equals into the developing institution of monasticism and was content for the majority to remain in patriarchally structured families. Nevertheless, the first theological reflection upon the saints retained the subversive non-familial heart of the gospel message. Brown demonstrates that by the middle of the fifth century it was very clear how the Christians regarded their saints: in the words of Bishop Theodoret of Cyrrhus a saint was an *aoratos philos* and a *gnesios philos*: an invisible and intimate *friend*. The language of friendship was applied to both saints and guardian angels in the first few centuries of Christianity's development. Indeed, with the Christianization of the patriarchal family, the friendship of saints offered people, particularly women, the only possibility of choice in their networks of relationship, as even St Ambrose noted.[43] St Augustine was of the opinion that the friendship of the saints was of more use than that of the angels because the saints were human beings and, unlike the angels, ruptured in their own persons the fault line between heaven and earth, divinity and humanity.[44] Brown believes that in the fourth century the language of friendship, when applied to the saints, was also the language of patronage borrowed from the social relations of the empire. The patron saint, much like the guardian angel, had a particularly close relationship with an individual, and would be particularly useful in pleading the individual's cause at the Last Judgement. As well as patron the saint was also an exemplar. In late antiquity, Brown points out, people went to persons to learn, not to institutions, and it was that person, rather than ideas or theories, who had the ability to mould an individual. Christianity theologized around these ideas, holding up saints not just as examples of 'good' humanity but as examples of God, revelations of the divine in human life.[45]

Brown cites as an example of the friendship relationship between saints the bond reported by St Gregory of Nyssa to have existed between his sister St Macrina and St Thecla. The latter was a first-century saint who has enjoyed considerable popularity down the centuries (but was one of the female saints whose cults were suppressed in 1969). Her story is told in the *Acts of Paul and Thecla*. She was converted to Christianity by St Paul and as a result took a vow of virginity, thus breaking off her engagement. Her parents handed her over to magistrates who had her tortured and Paul scourged and expelled from Iconium. Thecla managed super-naturally to resist all torment: animals (lionesses are specifically mentioned) refused to eat her, a storm doused the fire meant to consume her. This won her the admiration of many, particularly women, and one woman in particular, Tryphaena, a member of the imperial family, was converted to Christianity as a result. Thecla even baptized herself by jumping into a ditch. Eventually with the help of her noble friend she escaped persecution, donning male clothing for the purpose, and joined St Paul in Myra. He commissioned Thecla to teach and she spent the rest of her life doing that. The Thecla story was re-membered in the 1970s by Christian feminist scholars such as Schüssler Fiorenza and Ruether who argue that Thecla's story gives some insight into women's ministry in the early Church and also suggest that this work, despite its popularity, did not make it into the canon because of the patriarchalization of the Church – of which the fixing of the canon was a part.[46] In any case, Gregory of Nyssa relates that his sister had a secret name revealed to her by Thecla during her birth and that in a vision her mother was assured that she was giving birth to a second Thecla.

The language of patronage is a difficult one for feminists, implying as it does an unequal distribution of power between the parties involved and the dependence of one upon another (and associated as it is in Western culture with the 'old-boy network', men using power to support and advance each other at others' expense). But the language of friendship is a pearl of great price prised from the bin, a piece of cloth that fits perfectly into the patchwork. In searching for a model of relating that breaks the strait-jacket of patriarchal constructs of domination, dependence and submission in favour of mutuality, equality and interdependence, some Christian feminists have re-membered the concept of friendship, drawing upon the experience of women's friendships past and present. Theologians like Hunt, Heyward and myself have sought to centre friendship at the heart of all relating, 'sexual' and 'non-sexual', human and divine, believing that this concept is also at the heart of the gospel.

And so in the midst of the early development of a theology of sainthood which may seem to have little commend it to feminists, we have found two concepts that resonate with feminists, anti-dualism and friendship. It is with these two concepts that I propose to begin to work towards the fashioning of a feminist theology of sainthood.

NOTES

1 Margaret R. Miles, 'Introduction' in Clarissa W. Atkinson, Constance H. Buchanan and Margaret R. Miles, *Immaculate and Powerful: The Female in Sacred Image and Social Reality* (Boston: Beacon Press, 1985), pp. 3–4.

2 Linda Otto Lipsett, *Remember Me: Women and Their Friendship Quilts* (San Francisco: Quilt Digest Press, 1985), p. 30.

3 Mary E. Hunt, *Fierce Tenderness: A Feminist Theology of Friendship* (New York: Crossroad, 1991), p. 60.

4 Carter Heyward, *Touching Our Strength: The Erotic as Power and the Love of God* (San Francisco: Harper and Row, 1989), p. 138.

5 Mary Condren, *The Serpent and the Goddess: Women, Religion and Power in Celtic Ireland* (San Francisco: HarperSanFrancisco, 1989), pp. 65–78.

6 See Susan Haskins, *Mary Magdalen: Myth and Metaphor* (London: HarperCollins, 1993).

7 Karen Scott, 'St Catherine of Siena "Apostola"', *Church History*, vol. 61 (March 1992), pp. 34–46.

8 Barbara Corrado Pope, 'A heroine without heroics: the Little Flower and her times', *Church History*, vol. 57 (March 1988), p. 50.

9 J. W. Conn, 'Thérèse of Lisieux from a feminist perspective', *Spiritual Life*, vol. 28 (Winter 1982), pp. 234–6.

10 Conn, 'Thérèse of Lisieux from a feminist perspective', p. 235.

11 Sean Kelly and Rosemary Rogers, *Saints Preserve Us!* (London: Robson Books, 1995), pp. 265–6.

12 Conn, 'Thérèse of Lisieux from a feminist perspective', p. 236.

13 Leonard Feeney SJ, *Elizabeth Seton: An American Woman* (New York: America Press, 1938).

14 Mary Collins OSB, 'Daughters of the Church: the four Theresas', *Concilium*, no. 182 (1985), p. 22.

15 This was certainly the view of Victoria Sackville-West and explored in her classic study of this saint and Thérèse of Lisieux, *The Eagle and the Dove: A Study in Contrasts – St Teresa of Avila, St Thérèse of Lisieux* (London: Michael Joseph, 1943).

16 Sackville-West, *The Eagle and the Dove*, p. 65.

17 Mary Luti, '"A marriage well arranged": Teresa of Avila and Fray Jeronimo Gracián de la Madre de Dios', *Studia Mystica*, vol. 12 (Spring 1989), pp. 32–46.

18 Mother Ana de la Encarnación, cited in Mary Neill OP and Ronda Chervin, *Great Saints, Great Friends* (New York: Alba House, 1989), p. 82.

19 Elizabeth Usherwood, *Women First: Biographies of Catholic Women in the Forefront of Change* (London: Sheed and Ward, 1989), p. 40.

20 Collins, 'Daughters of the Church', p. 22.

21 Marina Warner, *Joan of Arc: The Image of Female Heroism* (London: Vintage, 1991), p. 6.

22 Warner, *Joan of Arc*, p. 6.

23 Warner, *Joan of Arc*, p. 145.

24 Neill and Chervin, *Great Saints, Great Friends*, p. 63.

25 Neill and Chervin, *Great Saints, Great Friends*, p. 63.

26 Warner, *Joan of Arc*, pp. 24–5.

27 Warner, *Joan of Arc*, p. 42.

28 Warner, *Joan of Arc*, p. 44.

29 Margaret Murray, *The Witch-Cult in Western Europe* (Oxford: Oxford University Press, 1921) and *The God of the Witches* (Oxford: Oxford University Press, 1952).

30 Warner, *Joan of Arc*, pp. 198–9.

31 Warner, *Joan of Arc*, p. 91.

32 For such an interpretation see Judy Grahn, *Another Mother Tongue: Gay Words, Gay Worlds* (Boston: Beacon Press, 1984), pp. 146–7.

33 Warner, *Joan of Arc*, pp. 218–36.

34 See for example Judy Grahn's description of Joan as 'a model dyke of high degree, a warrior-maid, the female Puck, a ceremonial butch, Maid of God, and a woman with whom many Lesbians have identified' in her highly contentious gay cultural history, *Another Mother Tongue*, p. 147.

35 Kelly and Rogers, *Saints Preserve Us!*, p. 153.

36 Elizabeth Stuart, *Just Good Friends: Towards a Lesbian and Gay Theology of Relationships* (London: Mowbray, 1995), pp. 1–27.

37 Cited in Gilbert Márkus OP, *The Radical Tradition: Saints in the Struggle for Justice and Peace* (London: Darton, Longman and Todd, 1992), p. xiv.

38 Mary Grey, *The Wisdom of Fools? Seeking Revelation for Today* (London: SPCK, 1993).

39 Peter Brown, *The Cult of the Saints: Its Rise and Function in Latin Christianity* (London: SCM, 1981).

40 Brown, *The Cult of the Saints*, p. 30.

41 Stuart, *Just Good Friends*, pp. 163–8.

42 Brown, *The Cult of the Saints*, p. 35.

43 Brown, *The Cult of the Saints*, p. 44.

44 Brown, *The Cult of the Saints*, p. 61.

45 Peter Brown, 'The saint as exemplar in late antiquity' in John Stratton Hawley (ed.), *Saints and Virtues* (Berkeley: University of California Press, 1987), pp. 3–14.

46 This view is vigorously disputed by Lynne C. Boughton in her article, 'From pious legend to feminist fantasy: distinguishing hagiographical license from apostolic practice in the *Acts of Paul/Acts of Thecla*', *Journal of Religion*, vol. 71 (1991), pp. 362–83. Boughton demonstrates a remarkable lack of awareness of gender issues in the early Church and in the writing of theology and history. She assumes that the male presentation of Christian history is factual and therefore her arguments are not convincing to a feminist.

3

Strange friendship:
women and saints

Can the concept of friendship that apparently lay behind the earliest articulation of a theology of sainthood be recycled into a feminist theology of sainthood? This is the question to which I now turn. I want to begin by examining the relationship between women and their saints to draw out the strands that constitute that relationship. We begin with the well-documented relationship between Joan of Arc and her three saintly companions, St Margaret of Antioch, St Katherine of Alexandria and St Michael.

We learn of Joan's relationship to her 'voices' from the trial records. In every single session the subject of the voices was debated. Were they from God or from the devil, who was capable of the most ingenious disguises? No one doubted that the wall between heaven and earth was breachable, but the gates of hell were also firmly ajar. Apart from the trial records there are also accounts of Joan's voices from her contemporaries. Perceval de Boulainvilliers, a courtier of Charles VII, wrote to the Duke of Milan in 1429, extolling the virtues of this woman sent by God. He relates that Joan's first heavenly call came when she was playing with friends in the fields around Domrémy. A youth appeared and told her to go home to her mother. Her mother, however, claimed not to have sent any messenger and Joan returned to her friends. In the fields a bright cloud came down before her and a voice spoke from it: 'Joan, you must lead another life and perform wondrous deeds; for you are she whom the King of Heaven has chosen to bring reparation to the kingdom of France and help and protection to King Charles.' The voice ceased, the cloud withdrew and Joan was left stunned.[1] The 'apparitions' which continued are never given any identity or physical form in Boulainvilliers' account, they are simply acknowledged to be divine. Dunois, bastard of Orleans, who fought alongside Joan, gave evidence at her rehabilitation in 1456 which differs both from Boulainvilliers' account and from Joan's answers during her trial. He claimed that Joan saw St Louis and Charlemagne, patrons of France, praying for the safety of the king and the city of Orleans. Guy de Cailly who also fought with Joan and put her up at his castle was believed by the king to have shared Joan's visions which were of unidentified angels.[2] Apart from Dunois, none of those who spoke at her rehabilitation trial identify her voices, except to confirm that they believed they came from God and not another source. In fact the voices were played down at her rehabilitation. At her trial Joan kept referring her inquisitors to the previous examination of her vocation made at King Charles's request at Poitiers to determine whether this woman had been genuinely sent to him from God. The records from this examination do not survive but witnesses at her other trials mentioned the proceedings at Poitiers. The problem is that they testify to the fact that her virginity, her birth and family and childhood, as well as her conduct, were all subject to examination, but no mention is made of her voices. Warner concludes that all this evidence points to the facts that 'before her trial, Joan did not speak of her voices in the same terms as she used during it'.[3] Warner believes that the explanation for this lies in the fact that during her trial Joan adopted the language of her hostile inquisitors to articulate her experience and this was a fatal mistake, for they were

> obsessed with determining the extent of Joan's sensual experience of her voices, the extent of her bodily contact with them, the nature of their physical manifestation. If they could not prove her pollution by association with earthly beings, they would through her tangible experience of the other world. Joan was their plaything, she was lured into a gin she did not even understand to be there, which bit into her deeper and deeper as she struggled to express her truth in a language that she would not fully master and would yet be intelligible to her questioners. As they were adept in branches of learning she hardly knew by name, she took her lead from them, borrowed their images to render explicit the ineffable. The trap into which they prodded her closed inexorably.[4]

Whether this is the only explanation of the discrepancies is an issue that will have to be examined. Joan gave her account of her original call at the second public session. She related how, at the age of thirteen, in her father's garden during the summer, she heard a voice emanating from the direction of her village church accompanied by a bright light. She identified it as an angel's, which told her of her vocation. She also insisted that her visions were shared with her friends, including the king. Yet right from the beginning Joan mixes her pronouns, sometimes referring to 'the' or 'this' voice, sometimes to 'them'. From then on Joan had to engage in a battle of wits with her inquisitors. They asked her an endless stream of questions, such as, did the voices have eyes? She usually refused to answer, on the grounds that she did not have permission to do so. It was in the fourth session that Joan, in response to more hostile questioning, named Sts Katherine and Margaret, saying that they had appeared to her 'crowned richly and beautifully' and asserting that she had God's permission to reveal this. She refused to elaborate with descriptions of the saints, referring her interrogators to her examination at Poitiers, although she did reveal that she did not recognize them immediately, adding rather mysteriously 'I knew them well enough once, but I have forgotten'.[5]

Then she began to talk about St Michael and revealed that it was Michael who first visited her, his presence bringing 'great comfort'. In response to questioning she said that she saw the saints before her eyes surrounded by angels: 'I saw them with my bodily eyes as well as I see you; and when they left me, I wept; and I would have had them take me with them, too.'[6] She went on to say that Margaret had comforted her when she was wounded, and that she had expected to be injured because Katherine and Margaret had told her she would be. During the last two public sessions she became uncooperative and impatient with the questioning, producing the assertive replies about Margaret's language and Michael's clothing that were quoted in the previous chapter. She would reveal only that she heard them several times during every day, that they spoke in beautiful voices, sweet and low, and that they brought her great joy. In subsequent interrogations in her cell she told her questioners in response to questions that she had embraced the feet of Katherine and Margaret, that they smelt good and that they were warm to the touch.

Joan's voices were her downfall. Her judges concluded that her relationships with her saints 'seem to partake of idolatry and to proceed from a pact made with devils'.[7] The reasons given were that, since even Mary the Mother of God did not receive such 'reverence or greetings' from archangels, Joan's claims must be 'presumptuous, rash, deceitful' and all her claims must be 'lies invented by Joan, suggested or shown to her by the demon in illusive apparitions, in order to mock at her imagination while she meddled with things that are beyond her and superior to the faculty of her condition'.[8] She also failed to report any 'sign sufficient to know them by' and had not sought the confirmation of the validity of her vision from any bishop or priest. So in essence Joan's sin was to trust in her own experience, to seek no ecclesiastical approval for her experience and to refuse to justify her experience to her interrogators. Warner maintains that her description of her visions, largely formed in the language of her interrogators which she attempted to resist, identified her with witchcraft because they were too 'down to earth', too human. For example, it was believed that witches would embrace a devil during their Sabbat ceremonies starting with his feet and then moving onto his genital region. He took on flesh to appear to them but was completely cold to the touch. Joan, like thousands of women in the Middle Ages, fell foul of an ongoing church debate over how the divine manifests itself in the world. Joan's judges were clear that humanity and divinity were completely and utterly different substances and one could not transform itself into another. Only the dark side of the supernatural could perform the devilish act of mixing or switching natures, muddying the waters of a highly ordered and stratified universe. 'Demons farted, stank, gabbled and generally aped the fashion of the world; saints and angels soared far above the bodily metaphors that could capture them for human reality.'[9] Others influenced by Neoplatonism maintained that spirits could assume human form to engage in conversation with humans. A year before Joan met her fate, one of her supporters, a Breton woman named Pieronne, was burned for witchcraft for reporting very physical visions of God, who according to the report of the Bourgeois de Paris 'often appeared to her in human form and talked to her as one friend does to another', and indeed the last time she saw him he was 'wearing a long white robe, and a red one underneath'. She also admitted to taking communion twice in one day, then a sin. Joan was also known to take communion often, daily if possible – something extremely rare in her day because a person had to be in a state of grace, an extremely difficult state to attain. Her accusers were suspicious of this practice. By taking communion whilst wearing male clothes they thought she was making a dangerous mockery out of the sacrament and perverting its power in order to strengthen her own devilish skills. Warner is clear that Joan died because she

> did not respect divisions, did not sift and classify according to the given laws of appropriateness. Her saints have bodies, talk French, wear clothes and can be held and touched. She could not see the incongruity – why should the soul not have ears and eyes? All unwittingly, she trespassed against a basic structural axiom in the Christian idea of the holy and sinned both against the classical idea of propriety,

that abstractions should remain abstract and not take on material shape, and against the strong enduring strain of Platonic idealism, which decrees that all things have their appropriate nature. Always artlessly, Joan displayed a profound and unerring ability to cross from the permitted to the impermissible and thus to define others' fears and assumptions, until the clarity became unbearable and she became a victim of her own illumination.[10]

Warner believes that Joan picked the figures of Michael, Katherine and Margaret from around her to express, under considerable pressure from her judges, in literal terms the non-literalness of her vision:

> There is nothing derogatory to Joan in this; it would reveal the same unsubtle literal-mindedness of her interrogators to find Joan false because she expressed herself, under duress, according to what she knew. She reached for metaphors that would be so close to her experience that the distinction between truth and its simulacrum would be effaced. Michael, Catherine and Margaret were approxima- tions – hence the ambivalence about their appearance and the many references to an unnamed angel as well – but even as approximations, they came so close to rendering what she felt about her voices, that at times, when she talks of the consolation they bring her, she speaks with clear conviction.[11]

Whether Joan was conscious of this process Warner does not make clear. She does go on to note how loyal she was to these voices, firmly ascribing everything good and nothing bad to them. She also notes that Joan never internalized her experience, these voices were most certainly other than Joan, external to her: 'their identities never merge. It was a dynamic relationship, not a symbiosis.'[12] So externalized were the voices that their noise could be drowned out by human rowdiness.

Sts Michael, Margaret and Katherine were certainly familiar figures in fifteenth-century piety. Margaret and Katherine, as we have previously noted, were two of the Fourteen Holy Helpers. Margaret of Antioch was the daughter of a pagan priest who drove her out of her home when she converted to Christianity. She lived with her maid as a shepherdess until she attracted the attention of the governor of Antioch, Olybrius, who relentlessly pursued her, inflict- ing many horrendous persecutions which Margaret resists and sur- vives by inverting the experience. When she is immersed in a vat of water she prays that it will become a baptism to bind her closer to Christ, and a dove (the symbol of the Holy Spirit) appears, her bonds break and she bursts out of the vat singing.[13] When she is burned with torches, the fire becomes the fire of divine love and of the Holy Spirit sanctifying her. But the most memorable aspect of Margaret's persecution is her consumption by a dragon. Margaret even triumphs over this complete envelopment and bursts out of the dragon's belly. The demon who confronts her after her resurrection from the dragon draws attention to the light that emanates from her: 'Woman, you're not at all like other women. It seems to me that you shine brighter than the sun – but especially your body, which blazes with light.' Margaret responds in some medieval versions of her life with a self-affirming song of victory, 'I have thrown down the dragon . . . I am champion'.[14] However, Margaret and the many she converted to Christianity were beheaded during the Diocletian persecutions. According to many versions of her life, before she died she promised that those who read or wrote her life would receive an unfading crown in heaven and those who invoked her on their deathbed would receive divine protection from demons. The prayers of those who built churches in her honour would be answered, and women who prayed to her would be safe in childbirth as would their babies. These patronages both testify to and explain her immense popularity in the medieval period.

There are clearly certain elements in Margaret's story that resonate with Joan's. Here was someone who resisted marriage and endured horrendous persecution by men because of her independence as a woman. She was often depicted, sword in hand, pinning the dragon down. Warner reports that in one of the versions of her life Margaret is conflated with St Pelagia whose feast day she shared. Pelagia, also of Antioch, was a dancer converted by Bishop Nonnus of Edessa who saw her act and preached a sermon upon it which she heard. After being baptized and giving away her wealth she travelled to Jerusalem where she assumed male clothing and lived the rest of her life as a male hermit, 'Pelagius the beardless monk'. Obviously, the donning of male apparel would have further resonances with Joan's story.

Katherine of Alexandria was a fourth-century noblewoman, the daughter of a pagan king Costus. As a child Katherine demonstrated outstanding virtue and learning, her wisdom surpassing that of her teachers. After her father's death, Katherine refused to marry, announcing that she was preserving her virginity for an ideal husband. Many suitors pursued her, including the son of the Roman emperor. When she rejected him she feared danger and fled into the desert where she was drawn to a hermit, Adrian, who told her of

Christ. That night Katherine dreamt of Christ but his face was turned from her. The next day she was baptized and in a dream that night she was married to Christ and awoke to found a ring on her finger. Katherine returned to Alexandria and converted her people. She resumed her rule. The emperor, Maxentius, then ordered the destruction of Christianity in Alexandria. Katherine went before him to argue against him. He summoned fifty of his wisest men to dispute with her, but Katherine confounded every argument they put forward and all converted to Christianity, paying with their lives. Maxentius then began to make sexual advances towards Katherine, who resisted them claiming that Christ was her lover and only spouse. Maxentius then had horrific tortures meted out upon Katherine, who still managed to convert the empress and a Roman general with her powers of argument. Maxentius then subjected Katherine to even crueller torture. She was placed between two wheels each embedded with knives which moved in opposite directions. However, an angel descended and struck the wheel sending its parts flying into the crowds, killing several people. The empress then intervened to plead Katherine's cause and she was executed, her breasts being pulled from her body with iron forks. The general who tried to intervene to save her was also martyred. Katherine continued to reject the emperor's advances and was eventually beheaded. Catherine Innes-Parker notes that the imagery of battle is used throughout the text of Katherine's lives.[15] Like Margaret, Katherine was a hugely popular saint in the Middle Ages, particularly among women and especially those who were unmarried. She represented autonomy, learning, courage and resistance, and was frequently portrayed reading a book whilst standing upon the crushed wheel, but she also sometimes carried a sword, the symbol of her beheading. She was the patron of philosophers, students, young girls, universities, librarians and wheelwrights. But because her feast fell just before the beginning of Advent, when weddings were forbidden, ironically she was also invoked in the process of finding a husband quickly. Katherine and Joan have in common their autonomy and resistance to the powerful and 'wise', and the help of angels. Warner makes much of the contrast between Katherine and Margaret, pointing out that Alexandria was the centre of allegorical studies of the Bible, a great centre of learning and interpretation which had tended to emphasize the divinity of Christ over his humanity. Antioch was also a centre of learning but much more literalist in its reading of the Bible and tended to emphasize the humanity of Christ – in the early

Church these two places represented the two great philosophical traditions of Christianity and were often in debate. She goes on to note that Margaret was associated with motherhood, Katherine with virginity. However, the similarities between the saints outweigh the differences: they both resist marriage, leave home and live autonomous lives until captured by a hostile power, which they resist with supernatural help for just long enough to demonstrate the weakness of that power. Both emerge as champions, leaving their male oppressors looking foolish as many follow the example of the women. It is easy to understand why these two women were natural friends to Joan.

I am slightly uncomfortable with Warner's thesis that Joan was forced to identify her voices and speak of them in embodied terms because she was under pressure from her opponents. This is certainly one way of reading the evidence. But this may play into the hands of dualism. Warner assumes that the original experience of the voice was disembodied and utterly ineffable in human terms. Yet this is to ignore the evidence of the female mystics throughout the Middle Ages. It is a characteristic of medieval female mystics that their visionary experiences were thoroughly embodied. Giles Milhaven believes that the emphasis throughout the Middle Ages on the doctrine of the incarnation and therefore on the sacraments created a spiritual environment of embodiment which could lead mystics, some male but especially female, to describe being held by Christ, kissed by him and having their bodies impressed with his imprint.[16] As Benedicta Ward notes in her study of Hildegard and Teresa of Avila, women mystics managed to hold together experiences which Warner and most modern (and indeed ancient) commentators would regard as fundamentally dualistic. They knew that their visionary experiences took them beyond their usual bodily senses and that they experienced a reality beyond the capture of human language; yet that experience *was* felt in and expressed in the body. These bodily experiences 'were not seen as improper but as authenticating. Where people were peculiarly open to God it was expected that the effect would show in their bodies' through taste, smell, touch and hearing.[17]

Warner cites some of Teresa of Avila's writings on her own mystical experiences, such as her statements that divine words 'are not heard with the physical ear' and that perception of the divine presence is like a blind person's perception, but Teresa also experienced her visions in a deeply embodied form. Most famously, she described an angel piercing her heart with a fire-tipped golden spear which left her moaning with pain and afire with a great love of God. Despite the accusations of her opponents, Teresa never taught that human beings could or should, in the highest levels of contemplative prayer, abandon their own humanity or the humanity of Christ: 'We are not angels and we have bodies. It is quite ridiculous to play the angel while we are on earth.' She believed it was possible for the mind to disengage from the world of bodily images and experiences for very brief periods of time, but this carried dangers of a loss of humility and loss of devotion to the sacraments. For Teresa the liturgy was incredibly important, even in the highest realms of prayer, grounding and inspiring it. Whilst at Mass for the feast of St Paul she saw the resurrected Christ. On other occasions she was shown Christ's hands and face – the hands and face of a glorified body. On St Peter's day she 'sensed' but did not see Christ beside her and the vision was full of light, an invisible light of a knowledge 'brighter than the sun'.[18] Joan's hesitancy in answering questions about her visions and her use of two sets of language to speak about them – non-corporeal and corporeal – may not be due to her falling into a trap set for her by the men who questioned her but may simply reflect the common experience of women mystics in the Middle Ages that there was no fundamental incompatibility between divine and bodily experience. This is what can make these women so appealing to Christian feminists. Joan, who shared with most medieval women mystics a great devotion to the Eucharist, the continuing embodiment of Christ, defends the physical reality of her saints with as much passion as she refuses to describe them in detail. Both responses are a defence of the same mystical experience.

What is very obvious from the trial records is that Joan considered it inappropriate to discuss her saints with her judges. She only revealed their identity when she had special permission from God to do so and only divulged details subsequently with enormous reluctance. Her relationship with them was intensely private, not in the sense of being exclusively personal to herself (for she believed others participated in the experience, at least in the early days of her mission), but in being so intimately bound up with her mission that she did not feel her enemies had any right to interrogate them through her. The saints/voices were her motivating force, the energy behind her extraordinary actions, her authority in Carter Heyward's definition of that word, based upon the Latin root *augere*, which means 'to grow'. For Heyward authority is 'that which calls into being "something" that is already and, for that reason, can be trusted. The reason we can trust the authority of the story, or resource or person is that it does not impose an extraneous set of expectations upon us but rather evokes "something" we already know, or have or are.'[19] Heyward goes on to argue that such authority is fundamentally relational, it binds people into right relationship with one another.

This definition is fundamentally different from the patriarchal construction of authority as a hierarchical cascade of power, but it is a definition of authority that illuminates Joan's story. We know virtually nothing about Joan before her voices came to her but there is nothing to suggest that they prompted a complete character change in the woman, they simply augmented characteristics that were already there: an ambitious self-confident woman who was proud of the fact that she was not a cowherd but a spinner, which ranked higher in the social stratification of her day, and who did not even consider telling her parents of her vocation for she knew they would do all in their power to prevent her.[20] Joan never gave the impression that her voices forced her to do anything against her will – on the contrary, what they bring her most is great comfort and joy, some kind of confirmation that she is doing the right thing, some kind of approval. Theirs is a relationship in which Joan's friendship with her saints enables her to be herself, to become herself in a context which would not normally allow such a thing to happen. She becomes a female knight, leading armed forces. But it is also a relationship of challenge. She reported that they instructed her not to jump off the tower of Beaurevoir Castle but she disobeyed them and did so, in an attempt to escape from the hands of the English to whom she had just been sold. (It may have been a suicide attempt – this was certainly one of the interpretations offered by her judges; the other was that like all witches she thought she could fly[21]) St Katherine was particularly angry and told Joan to confess her sin. When, four days after abjuring, her assessors found her once again wearing male dress, she confirmed that it was her voices who had told her to resume it and that she had only signed the documents of recantation for fear of the fire. Her voices recalled her to her authenticity. So although it was often comforting it was not a comfortable friendship that Joan enjoyed with her saints. Closely linked in the mind of both Joan's judges and herself were her dress and her voices. Her voices gave her the strength she needed to defy concepts of womanhood and therefore concepts of nature and order in the world in which she lived. And although it is the trial record, not Joan herself, which explicitly states that it was on the instruction of Katherine and Margaret that she assumed male clothes, it is clear that Joan regarded the wearing of the clothes as an essential part of her mission.[22]

The characteristics of Joan's friendship (not a word she used herself) with her saints are as follows:

- She experienced them as embodied yet also as beyond normal human experience.
- They were clearly recognized characters with individual identities and voices.
- It was a dynamic relationship that she enjoyed with them: she felt able to argue against them and to ignore their advice.
- It was a relationship which enhanced Joan, building upon what was already in her character, and a relationship which drove her into what she believed to be right relationship with her people and country.
- It was a subversive relationship that enabled her to transcend and burst asunder the assumptions and stratifications of her society.
- It was a comforting relationship but not a comfortable one and not one that ultimately saved her. She let them down and they let her down, St Katherine promising an escape that never came.[23]

We see in Joan's experience of her relationship with her saints many of the characteristics of friendship identified by feminist theologians and philosophers in recent years:

- Friendship between women is subversive of what Janice Raymond has called 'hetero-reality' or patriarchy, which defines women solely in terms of their relationship to men. When women form friendships with each other they therefore rattle the foundations of patriarchy and this is why so much effort has gone into disparaging and devaluing female friendship.[24]
- Friendship is a voluntary relationship based upon mutuality and equality which is also inclusive and teaches us about interconnectedness with all life. Mary Hunt defines friendship as 'those voluntary human relationships that are entered into by people who intend one another's well-being and who intend that their love relationship is part of a justice-seeking community'.[25] It is about solidarity in the midst of difference, it is formed on the basis of common experience but acknowledges and celebrates diversity.
- Friendship is often experienced as grace – it is not sought and can often not be explained or artificially manufactured.

- Friendship is embodied and passionate. It is not, as often seems to be the case in some male understandings of friendship, the antidote or antithetical to sexual relationships.[26]
- Friendship is not a luxury amongst women and other groups of people who are marginalized and disempowered by the societal structures in which their lives are placed. For these people friendship is an essential part of the struggle for survival: it is the only place where people can find the safety to be vulnerable to each other, to discover a shared humanity and shared dreams, a discovery that empowers resistance and defiance. It is not an inherently rare relationship or necessarily enjoyed with only one person at a time.
- Friendship, whilst providing a survival space in the midst of patriarchal structures and a centre for resistance, is not itself a magical forest of 'perfection'. Friendships go wrong and end because the people involved in them have been taught to relate to others in a context of wrong-relationship. It is always difficult to dismantle learned behaviour in order to learn how to engage in right-relationship.
- Friendship is 'revelatory'. It both teaches us something about ourselves and provides us with a glimpse of something of the nature of God.

In an interesting essay on Christine de Pisan, Kevin Brownlee has sought to demonstrate how Joan of Arc enabled Christine to re-discover her voice as a female author. Christine had had to take refuge in a convent and had ceased to write, following the Anglo-Burgundian invasion of Paris. Joan's appearance in 1429 enabled Christine to end eleven years of silence. But there was also a metaphorical dimension:

> In the *Ditié [de Jehanne d'Arc]*, the figure of Joan of Arc is portrayed as a holy female warrior, a combination of Joshua and Deborah. Joan of Arc's appearance authorises the authorial voice of Christine de Pisan, who both bears witness to Joan's fulfilment of earlier prophecies and makes her own prophecies concerning the future of the Maid. Joan as God's chosen warrior thus authorises Christine to speak as a new prophet figure, a new Ezekiel or Isaiah.[27]

Brownlee charts a similar dynamic working in Christine de Pisan's *Cité des dames*, which was her reply to the misogynistic writings of her own day. In particular Christine focused on the story of St Christine. Christine structures her narrative around three of her

saint's persecutors: her father Urban does everything in his power
to dissuade the twelve-year-old girl from Christianity and a vow of
virginity, even to the extent of attempting to drown her, but her 'real'
heavenly father intervenes and enables her to walk upon water. The
water is no longer the water of death but the water of baptism. Christ
himself names the girl as 'Christine' after himself; previously she
is referred to only as 'daughter'. Here Christine de Pisan is rewriting
her sources in order to emphasize the saint's authorization. Urban
dies at the hand of the devil and a second persecutor emerges – the
judge Dyon who tortures her and attempts to make her worship
the idol of Jupiter. Christine commands the evil spirit to leave the
idol, which it does. She prays that the idol be reduced to dust and
it is, with the result that 3,000 male spectators are converted
and Dyon goes mad and dies. The third persecutor is another judge
– Julian. He cannot even make the saint's body move, a fire surrounds
her body, snakes refuse to bite her, she resurrects a snake killed in
the process. He then attempts to silence the saint because her power
obviously resides in her voice. Her tongue is cut out but she continues to be able to speak, praying to be taken to her God, and a
divine voice declares that she will indeed be rewarded for being so
faithful to the name of Christ. Julian has her tongue cut shorter but
she simply spits it into his face and continues to speak. She is then
put to death. Christine de Pisan finishes the story with a prayer to St
Christine, in which 'the miraculous voicing of the martyred female
saint is . . . presented as an empowering model for the voicing of the
female writer . . . By means of articulating St Christine's story –
about the spiritual empowerment of the female voice – the power of
Christine de Pisan's authorial voice is simultaneously demonstrated
and authorised.'[28] Christine de Pisan found in her saintly namesake
and in a saint-to-be authorization to be herself, a female author,
a voice of resistance against the misogyny of her day, and a voice of
encouragement to her female contemporaries.

Although we generally do not have as detailed access to the
friendship between other women and their saint-friends as we do
with Joan we can detect a similar pattern. Susan Haskins notes
that Mary Magdalen became a friendly saintly figure to many of the
medieval women mystics.[29] We have already noted that Catherine
of Siena felt a particular bond with this saint. Raymond of Capua
located Magdalen's influence in her guise of perfect penitent.
According to Raymond, when Catherine's sister died in childbirth,
which was interpreted as a punishment for her attempts to divert

Catherine from her vocation to virginity, Catherine was full of
remorse and cast 'herself down at the feet of our Lord with Mary
Magdalen', weeping and begging for mercy and hoping to hear the
words that Jesus had addressed to Mary: 'Thy sins are forgiven thee.'
According to Raymond she received her assurance and thereafter had
a particular devotion to Mary Magdalen and devoted her life to the
penitent acts of fasting, prayer and silence. In fact he portrays her
as a model nun – an enclosed contemplative. However, as Karen
Scott has pointed out, Catherine was not an enclosed nun, she was a
Dominican tertiary living in the world and very much involved in it.
Scott notes that Catherine 'did not stress the unusual elements in her
life – for example, it was not she who told stories about miraculous
cures, her mystical marriage, and her stigmata. She believed that she
was guided in her speaking by God, but she did not view her work
as supernatural in any extraordinary way.'[30] Scott locates Mary
Magdalen's influence in Catherine's self-definition as an apostle. We
have already noted that the explicit identification of Mary as an
apostle is a feature of the non-canonical gospels and it was revived in
the Middle Ages primarily by women, but it was the theologian
Peter Abelard who described Mary as the 'apostle to the apostles'.[31]
In Orthodox Christianity Mary Magdalen has always been acknowledged to be the first apostle/evangelist. Not only did the figure of
Mary endorse Catherine's chosen career as a travelling preacher and
ambassador but she also provided her with the strength to resist her
detractors and opponents. Catherine wrote to a female friend:

> If she [Mary Magdalen] had paid too much attention to herself, she
> would not have stayed [under the cross] with those people, Pilate's
> soldiers, and she would not have gone and remained alone at the tomb.
> Her love kept her from thinking: 'What impression will this make? Will
> they say bad things about me, because I am beautiful and of great
> importance?' She does not think such things, but only how she can
> find and follow her Master . . . She knew the path [to holiness] so well
> that she has become our spiritual master.[32]

Also like Magdalen in the non-canonical gospels, Catherine became
an apostle to apostles, a 'mother' to a group of priests, religious, lay
people and politicians. Like Joan, Catherine's sense of authority
came not from the institutional Church but from her own sense of
vocation (also, like Joan's, deeply rooted in her childhood), her direct
call and guidance from the divine, and the solidarity of Mary
Magdalen as apostle and fellow 'loose woman' – for, as Scott points

out, 'Women were forbidden to preach; and women "on the loose" were considered "loose women"'.[33] Indeed, Raymond relates that when Christ once appeared to Catherine he granted her unspoken request to be given Mary Magdalen (and not his mother Mary who was also present) as a second mother. And from what we know of Catherine's childhood, it is most certainly a case of building upon a character already there – the stubborn little girl locked in constant battle with her parents over her sense of vocation and her refusal to marry.

Mary Magdalen also plays a role in the story of Christina of Markyate (*c.* 1097–1161), whose life was written shortly after her death by an anonymous monk of St Albans who knew her. She was the daughter of a noble Anglo-Saxon family who lived in Huntingdon. She was baptized Theodora. In 1112 during a visit to St Albans Abbey the girl made a vow of virginity and changed her name to Christina to indicate that she now belonged to Christ alone. From that point on Christina resisted all suitors and particularly resisted her parent's strenuous efforts to marry her to Burthred. At first the Bishop of Lincoln upheld the validity of her vow of virginity but then succumbed to a bribe from her father and withdrew his protection. Christina was put under house arrest by her parents and forcibly married to Burthred, but still she resisted consummation of the union she had not consented to. She attempted to persuade her husband to adopt a chaste marriage, following the example of another female saint who enjoyed considerable popularity in the Middle Ages – St Cecilia. Cecilia was a third-century Roman martyr who, although she had taken a vow of virginity, was betrothed to the pagan Valerian. On their wedding night Cecilia explained the situation, adding that if Valerian attempted to consummate the marriage an angel would strike him. Valerian demanded to see the angel and was told this was only possible if he converted to Christianity and was baptized. He did this and saw the angel with his wife. She also converted her brother-in law who with her husband and herself was soon martyred. Unfortunately this story had no effect upon Burthred and Christina fled, dressed as a man and helped by a hermit who had consulted the Archbishop of Canterbury about her case. She went to live with Alfwen, an anchoress, for a couple of years and then she moved to a hermitage at Markyate under the protection of a hermit called Roger. In 1122 her marriage was declared to be cancelled by the Archbishop of York. She thereafter became a highly influential figure, visited by the high and lowly. What is interesting about the story of Christina is that she continued to have strong sexual urges. It is recorded that in a time of sexual temptation Christ came to her and she held him as a mother a child to her chest. Mary Magdalen intervened in Christina's life when she was attracted to an unnamed cleric whose protection she was under and who reciprocated her feelings. One night John the Evangelist, Benedict and Mary Magdalen appeared to the cleric in his sleep:

> Of these, Mary, for whom the priest had a particular veneration, glared at him with piercing eyes, and reproached him harshly for his wicked persecution of the chosen spouse of the most high King. And at the same time, she threatened him that if he troubled her any further he would not escape the anger of the almighty God and eternal damnation.[34]

The priest was duly chastened and begged Christina's pardon. She too went into the wilderness to attempt to rid herself of her feelings towards this man. In Christina's story, then, St Cecilia provides her with a way to redeem a violent situation enforced upon her against her will, but lets her down. Her determination in alliance with the commitment of her friends to help her realize her vocation (which again is sealed in childhood) enables her to achieve what she desires in the end, but this involves defying family and Church. Mary Magdalen figures in her life as an uncomfortable friend, intervening in the midst of a relationship to recall Christina to her vocation.

An interesting relationship developed between the English mystic Margery Kempe (c. 1373–1433) and Mary. Margery married and had fourteen children with her husband John. She then had some sort of breakdown and began to receive visions. In 1414 she and her husband took vows of chastity and Margery began to wear white, the symbol of purity and virginity. This habit annoyed many, but Margery was reassured by Christ in a vision that he 'loved wives also, and specially those wives who would live chaste if they might have their will . . . yet I love you daughter, as much as any maiden in the world', pointing out that many non-virgins including Mary Magdalen had found places in heaven.[35] For most of her life Margery felt she had taken the wrong path in life and regretted her marriage. There are two ways of reading this regret: one could argue that Margery's life was ruined by the dualism that infected Christianity which extolled virginity above marriage, thus leading her to believe that her life was second-class and her salvation in doubt. But it is also possible to read the story in a more positive way as Margery's search for independence in order to fulfil her vocation which was to draw attention to and weep for the sins of the world – a vocation which she was assured by the Virgin Mary in Jerusalem was endorsed by the example of Mary Magdalen. For Margery, Mary Magdalen was a sisterly figure sharing a deep personal relationship with Christ and distraught suffering at having to witness his pain – and her sisterly feeling sometimes boiled over into sibling rivalry as Margery meditated on Mary's privilege in handling the body of Christ.[36] But St Katherine of Alexandria and St Margaret were also friends to Margery. When she underwent a spiritual marriage to Christ she named these two saints and some other holy virgins as the chief witnesses.

Sts Katherine and Cecilia gave the tired and desperate Frideswide the strength to resist the violent advances of Algar, prince of Mercia, who ignored her vow of celibacy and relentlessly hunted her down.

Eva Catafygiotu Topping, in her discussion of the previously mentioned St Pulcheria who convened the Council of Chalcedon, noted that the empress convened the council in the basilica of the local female martyr St Euphemia because the empress was convinced that this martyr would support her in her efforts to establish what would later be labelled as 'orthodoxy': 'Thus the collaboration of two women, one in heaven and the other on earth, secured the success of the Council of Chalcedon and the triumph of Orthodoxy over heresy.'[37] Euphemia of Chalcedon was a fourth-century virgin and martyr. One tradition relates that she wore black clothes to indicate that she had renounced all worldly pleasure, but another tradition presents her as assuming the brown robes of a philosopher and indeed she became the patron not only of the Eastern Church but of the faculty of theology in Paris, indicating that a now obscured tradition knew her to be a philosopher/theologian. This helps to explain why the empress saw her as a friend in her own theological struggles. Two women form an alliance to intervene in matters that many men would have regarded to be beyond their capability or nature.

Elizabeth of Schönau, the friend of Hildegard of Bingen who also received visions and became leader of the women's section of her abbey, had a mutually supportive relationship with St Ursula whose cult she vigorously promoted. Ursula provided comfort and support in visions to Elizabeth who found her role as prophet extremely demanding. Ursula was a fourth-century princess, daughter of a

Christian king of Cornwall, Brittany or Ireland (the story varies). She wished to remain a virgin but was betrothed to a pagan prince, her father being reluctant to defy the wishes of another king. Ursula agreed to the marriage on three conditions: that the prince gave her ten virgins of the royal blood as companions and that each of these had one thousand attendants; that the marriage be delayed for three years so she and her companions could visit the shrines of the saints; that the prince and his court convert to Christianity. Much to her surprise he agreed. So Ursula and her eleven thousand women (she herself also had a thousand attendants) set out to Rome in eleven ships. Some clergy accompanied them but no sailors. The wind blew the ship into the Rhine, Ursula had a vision that they would be killed if they remained in Cologne so they sailed to Basle and then walked to Rome, angels assisting their transport over the Alps. On their arrival in Rome the Pope came to greet them, and Ursula's intended husband arrived the same day to reveal that he no longer wanted to be married but to be martyred for her faith. The Pope and some bishops joined Ursula on their boat back to Cologne where they were massacred by the Huns. Elizabeth was responsible for adding the detail about the Pope and cardinals accompanying Ursula on her journey to martyrdom. Ursula is usually depicted in royal garb sheltering her many companions under her cloak. Her story is given little historical credence by scholars and Elizabeth is blamed for adding to the story historically dubious elements which were fed to her by two abbots of Deutz.[38] But the appeal of Ursula to Elizabeth is obvious. She confided details of her life to a woman, trusted her with her memory, as those who made friendship quilts did, when those around Elizabeth often made her question her own convictions. Ursula became a popular saint among the mystics of northern Europe, a resisting woman who joined together with other women in order to pursue her own goal and avoid the control of men over her life; the highest placed man in the Church and his companions acknowledged her authority and followed her, even to their deaths. Ursula became a powerful symbol of the authority of religious women's autonomy.

One saint who did use the explicit language of friendship when speaking about her relationships with other saints was Thérèse of Lisieux. In her description of her pilgrimage to Italy, which is full of stories of her defying guides and barriers to touch, kiss and even steal relics from the holy places she visited, Thérèse recounted her encounter with St Cecilia:

After the Colosseum, we went to the catacombs. Céline and I managed to lie down together in what had once been the tomb of St Cecilia, and to scoop up some of the earth which her sacred remains had sanctified. I had no particular devotion to her before the pilgrimage, but after I had visited the house where she had been martyred, and heard her called the 'Queen of Harmony' because of the song she sang in her virginal heart to her Divine Spouse, it was more than devotion that I felt; it was the love of friendship; and she became my patroness and intimate confidante. What delighted me about her was the way she abandoned herself to God, and her unbounded confidence, which enabled her to purify souls who had never desired anything but the joys of the world.[39]

Thérèse was also able to visit the church of St Agnes, 'one of the friends of my childhood'. It is interesting that Thérèse was attracted to Cecilia because of her 'unbounded confidence'. What Agnes and Cecilia had in common was a unbreakable determination to fulfil their own destiny against the obstructions of others. Thérèse also possessed 'unbounded confidence' and determination which, a few days after meeting up with her saintly friends, would lead her to defy all protocol and speak to the Pope during an audience, begging his help in seeking to realize her vocation. Thérèse wanted it all, she wanted to be 'a warrior, a priest, an apostle, a doctor of the Church, a martyr'.[40] Her friendship with her female saints inspired, legitimized and fuelled that expansive vocation.

Carter Heyward has noted that some people have the power to see and call forth 'in us that spiritual power which we are born to share, generate, celebrate and pass on',[41] the sacred power of mutual relation, the subversive power of Sophia that chips away at the foundation of patriarchy, of wrong-relation, until all are liberated from them, until all are able to enjoy right-relation. It is that spiritual power that the female saints seemed to be able to call forth in other women. Theirs is not a relationship of patronage in the sense of being a privileged 'protector' and 'protected', it is a friendship that reinforces and conjures up a spirit or power already existing in the woman through a sense of solidarity. And it is too simplistic to state that the friendship lay in imitation and inspiration. Certainly there were similarities between Joan and the situations she faced and those of her saints, but these lay in generalities rather than particulars

Interestingly, Heyward goes on (in a sermon for the ordination of a gay priest) to identify 'four signs of sacred voices', in order that we can distinguish between God's voices and our own self-delusions, the voices which claim our allegiance but which do not merit it.

- 'The voices of God always call us more fully into *mutually empowering relationship* in which all parties are taken seriously and enabled more fully to be true selves.'[42] We have already noted that this is a clear characteristic of the relationship between women and their female saints – women are never diminished by the relationship, they are not coerced to do anything against their will, they are called to fulfil what is already within them. Nor is the relationship one way, top-down: Joan argues with her saints. Women often promoted the stories of their saints to others. It was a mutually beneficial arrangement.

- 'God speaks *embodied, sensual words*, their sources rich in human history and deep in the earth, our planet home.'[43] Much to the embarrassment of some contemporary and most modern commentators, relationships between saints and their friends could be embodied and yet also in some way beyond normal human contact.

- '*The voices of God are not solo voices.* God sings with and through us all.'[44] Feminism has for a long time drawn attention to the radical individualism that permeates capitalism and Protestantism, giving human beings the impression that they are on their own, in competition with others and that they need to struggle against others to survive. The relationship of women to their saints demonstrates that they are not 'on their own' but part of a common struggle that stretches back into the night of the past and forward into the morning mist of the future.

- 'Because the voices of God are seasoned in our commonness, our connectedness as a body of brothers and sisters, they are voices of *compassion*.'[45] Compassion involves recognizing our connectedness with our friends and enemies, refusing to give up on them, constantly challenging them whilst always recognizing our own need to repent of sins, our own imperfection. The saints seem to have often exercised a challenging function in their relationships with their friends, calling forth spiritual power but preventing the development of spiritual arrogance.

Heyward concludes her sermon with these words: 'Individuals will come and go. But the victory is being won because we are standing *together*, giving voices to a God who was with us in the beginning and will be with us in the end, staring us down and holding us up.'[46] This seems to come close to what friendship between different generations of women saints teaches us – the same struggle goes on with different players but the players can draw strength from each other and not only from contemporaries.

Jacobus de Voragine's *The Golden Legend* offers six reasons why saints should be honoured, reasons drawn from William of Auxerre:

- In doing so we honour the divine majesty, for it is God who made them saints.
- We need their help, for we cannot save ourselves.
- 'To increase our own sense of security – in other words, to have the glory of the saints recalled to us on their feast day, and thus to build up our own hope and confidence.'
- To encourage imitation.
- To 'pay the debt of interchanging neighbourhood'. The saints rejoice over our repentance, so we should celebrate their feasts. The relationship must be mutual and reciprocal.
- 'To assure our own honour, because when we honour the saints, we are taking care of our own interests and procuring our own honour. Their feast day honours us. When we pay tribute to our brothers, we honour ourselves, since love makes all things to be in common, and all things are ours, in heaven, on earth, and in eternity.'[47]

The theology of sainthood that emerges from these six points is one of comfort, familiarity, closeness, neighbourliness – friendship. Certainly there were understandings of sainthood around in late medieval Europe that were based upon feudal relationships – the relationship between the patron saint of a parish and the parish was 'essentially feudal, and the saint was bound by a sense of *noblesse oblige* towards those who paid him [*sic*] honour and financial tribute in the shape of tithe and wax'.[48] But Duffy points out that there is little evidence that there was much personal devotion to church patrons in late medieval England. People chose their own saintly friends for a variety of reasons, mostly to do with some sense of common feeling with the saint which was expressed in the iconography:

Julian of Norwich wrote of St John of Beverley, that 'oure lorde shewed hym full hyly in comfort of vs for homelynesse, and brought to my mynde how he is a kynd neyghbour and of our knowyng'. The saints who gazed benignly out from the screens and tabernacles of late medieval Englishmen were often emphatically 'kynd neyghbours and of our knowyng', country people themselves, like St James the Great at Westhall, in Suffolk, with his sensible shoes, hat, and staff, or St Anthony on the same screen, with his friendly pig, or St Sitha, alias

Zita of Lucca [a thirteenth-century Italian domestic servant who gave away her master's goods to the poor] at Barton Turf or Litcham All Saints or North Elmham, dressed in kerchief and apron, clutching her shopping-bag, keys, and rosary, like any hard-worked English housewife, to whom she was well known for her help in recovering lost property, especially the household keys.[49]

St Anne, mother of the Virgin Mary, was a very popular saint in late medieval England. Married to Joachim, Anne and her husband were righteous Jews but Joachim was thrown out of the Temple at Jerusalem because he was sterile. Too ashamed to go home, he went to live among shepherds. There he was visited by an angel who assured him that his wife would give birth to a girl who would in turn give birth to the Son of the Most High. Husband and wife were miraculously reunited at the Golden Gate of Jerusalem and a chaste embrace resulted in conception and subsequent birth of Mary who was brought up in the Temple as the angel instructed. Anne survived Joachim and went on to be remarried twice, producing two more daughters, Mary Salome (mother of James and John) and Mary Cleopas (mother of four more apostles). Anne is often portrayed on medieval rood screens surrounded by the Holy Kindred, Jesus' extended family. Anne represented maternity and fecundity and was naturally particularly dear to women. Her fecundity became something of an embarrassment to some contemporary and later male clerics. In the fifteenth century St Anne appeared to St Colette (whose life's work was to revise the rule of St Clare to return it to its original vision) and assured her that she had indeed been married three times.

But we have already noted that also particularly popular on the rood screens of medieval England were the virgin martyrs of earlier ages. These were surely not 'kynd neyghbours and of our knowyng', portrayed as they were with their instruments of torture. Duffy argues that the appeal of these women saints lay not in their appeal as *exemplars*, except for a few such as Margery Kempe and to those theologians who taught the superiority of the virginal state. Rather the appeal of these women lay in their power. 'Virginity as a symbol of sacred power, a concrete realisation within this world of the divine spirit, has a very ancient pedigree within Christianity . . . What it gave to the ordinary Christian man and woman was not so much a model to imitate, something most of them never dreamt of doing, but rather a source of power to be tapped.'[50] Their extraordinary resistance to persecution gave them a power, a particular closeness to

Christ which could be tapped, which explains the apparent oddity of virgin saints being invoked in connection with marriage and child-birth. The power of one type of woman could be drawn upon by another type of woman (or man). The friendship was not based upon imitation but on difference.

I took this detour into late medieval concepts of saints to demonstrate that the concept of friendship lay beneath the theology of sanctity then as it did in the early Church. Indeed, the closeness of saints to ordinary people is more emphasized in the late medieval period, by which time the doctrine of the Communion of Saints was fully developed. *The Golden Legend* reminds us that, in picking up on the *relationship* dimension of sainthood, a feminist theology of sainthood would not in fact be far from a traditional orthodox under-standing, but it also reminds us that there is much that grates with Christian feminism as it has developed in the twentieth century. How is a Christian feminist to explain the friendship between a long-dead woman and a living one? Is it possible to develop a concept of sainthood that does not ultimately dissolve into the dualism of disembodied souls and afterlives? To these questions we now turn. There are, I think, two approaches offered to a Christian feminist: one we might label a minimalist theology of sainthood, the other is a daring, risky flourish of a theology. In developing both approaches I will be stitching together patches of theology from a variety of feminist theologians.

NOTES

1 Marina Warner, *Joan of Arc: The Image of Female Heroism* (London: Vintage, 1991), p. 119.
2 Warner, *Joan of Arc*, p. 120.
3 Warner, *Joan of Arc*, p. 120.
4 Warner, *Joan of Arc*, p. 119.
5 Warner, *Joan of Arc*, p. 124.
6 Warner, *Joan of Arc*, p. 125.
7 Warner, *Joan of Arc*, p. 127.
8 Warner, *Joan of Arc*, pp. 127–8.
9 Warner, *Joan of Arc*, p. 130.
10 Warner, *Joan of Arc*, p. 136.
11 Warner, *Joan of Arc*, p. 131.
12 Warner, *Joan of Arc*, p. 131.
13 Catherine Innes-Parker, 'Sexual violence and the female reader: symbolic "rape" in the saints' lives of the Katherine group', *Women's*

Studies, vol. 24, no. 3 (1985), p. 209.

14 Innes-Parker, 'Sexual violence and the female reader', p. 211.

15 Innes-Parker, 'Sexual violence and the female reader', p. 213.

16 Giles Milhaven, 'A medieval lesson on bodily knowing: women's experience and men's thought', *Journal of the American Academy of Religion*, vol. 57, no. 2 (Summer 1989), pp. 344–7.

17 Benedicta Ward, *Signs and Wonders: Saints, Miracles and Prayers from the Fourth Century to the Fourteenth* (Aldershot: Variorum, 1992), p. 109.

18 N. D. O'Donoghue, 'The human form divine: St Teresa and the humanity of Christ' in Margaret A. Rees (ed.), *Teresa de Jesús and Her World* (Leeds: Trinity and All Saints' College, 1981), pp. 75–88.

19 Carter Heyward, *Touching Our Strength: The Erotic as Power and the Love of God* (San Francisco: Harper and Row, 1989), pp. 73–4.

20 Warner, *Joan of Arc*, p. 155.

21 Warner, *Joan of Arc*, p. 113.

22 Warner, *Joan of Arc*, p. 155.

23 Warner, *Joan of Arc*, p. 113.

24 Janice Raymond, *A Passion for Friends: Towards a Philosophy of Female Affection* (London: The Women's Press, 1986).

25 Mary E. Hunt, *Fierce Tenderness: A Feminist Theology of Friendship* (New York: Crossroad, 1991), p. 29.

26 For a full exploration of this dimension of friendship see my *Just Good Friends: Towards a Lesbian and Gay Theology of Relationships* (London: Mowbray, 1995).

27 Kevin Brownlee, 'Martyrdom and the female voice: Saint Christine in the *Cité des dames*' in Renate Blumenfeld-Kosinski and Timea Szell (eds), *Images of Sainthood in Medieval Europe* (Ithaca: Cornell University Press, 1991), pp. 134–5.

28 Kevin Brownlee, 'Martyrdom and the female voice', p. 130.

29 Susan Haskins, *Mary Magdalen: Myth and Metaphor* (London: Harper-Collins, 1993), pp. 181–91.

30 Karen Scott, 'St Catherine of Siena "Apostola"', *Church History*, vol. 61 (March 1992), p. 37.

31 Haskins, *Mary Magdalen*, pp. 221–2.

32 Scott, 'St Catherine of Siena "Apostola"', p. 42.

33 Scott, 'St Catherine of Siena "Apostola"', p. 40.

34 C. H. Talbot, *The Life of Christina of Markyate, a Twelfth Century Recluse* (Oxford: Oxford University Press, 1959), p. 117.

35 B. A. Windeatt, *The Book of Margery Kempe* (Harmondsworth: Penguin, 1985), pp. 65–6.

36 Haskins, *Mary Magdalen*, pp. 189–90.

37 Eva Catafygiotu Topping, *Holy Mothers of Orthodoxy* (Minneapolis: Light and Life, 1987), p. 76.

38 See e.g. the entry on Ursula in David Hugh Farmer, *The Oxford*

Dictionary of Saints (Oxford: Oxford University Press, 1978), p. 387 and the entry on Elizabeth in Michael Walsh (ed.), *Butler's Lives of the Saints* (Tunbridge Wells: Burns and Oates, 1985), p. 185.

39 Thérèse of Lisieux, *The Story of a Soul* (Wheathampstead: Anthony Clarke Books, 1951), p. 72.

40 Thérèse of Lisieux, *The Story of a Soul*, pp. 154–5.

41 Carter Heyward, *Staying Power: Reflections on Gender, Justice, and Compassion* (Cleveland: The Pilgrim Press, 1995), p. 50.

42 Heyward, *Staying Power*, p. 53.

43 Heyward, *Staying Power*, p. 54.

44 Heyward, *Staying Power*, p. 56.

45 Heyward, *Staying Power*, pp. 56–7.

46 Heyward, *Staying Power*, p. 58.

47 Jacobus de Voragine, *The Golden Legend: Readings on the Saints*, translated by William Granger Ryan, vol. 2 (Princeton: Princeton University Press, 1993), pp. 273–4.

48 Eamon Duffy, *The Stripping of the Altars: Traditional Religion in England 1400–1580* (New Haven: Yale University Press, 1992), pp. 161–2.

49 Eamon Duffy, 'Holy maydens, holy wyfes: the cult of women saints in fifteenth and sixteenth-century England' in W. J. Sheils and Diana Wood (eds), *Women in the Church: Papers Read at the 1989 Summer Meeting and the 1990 Winter Meeting of the Ecclesiastical History Society* (Oxford: Basil Blackwell, 1990), pp. 177–8.

50 Duffy, 'Holy maydens, holy wyfes', p. 189.

4

Two theologies of sainthood

The minimalist approach: a community of solidarity

The theologian Sharon Welch has woven together a feminist ethic which is grounded in women's stories and draws upon some of the main themes of Latin American liberation theology. I believe that her work may provide us with a theological framework into which we can build a feminist theology of sainthood. It is therefore worth considering her thought in some detail. She embraces post-modernism completely, accepting that the notions of universal or absolute truth are an essential part of oppressive regimes.[1] We are always tempted to seek security in an insecure world, and those with power and wealth have the means to shore up their concepts of absolute truth and impose them upon the rest of us, so the quest for absolute truth is always the quest for power. Even a quest for a universal consensus is dangerous because it is a 'continuation of the dream of domination'.[2] What is needed, she argues, is a quest for universal solidarity which always recognizes and listens to the voices of others, even if consensus cannot be reached. The God portrayed in traditional theism simply legitimates the quest for power by guaranteeing absolute truth. Liberation theologians seek not to uncover universal truths but to do something much more dangerous and revolutionary, they uncover memories:

> The dangerous memory expressed in liberation theology is not only a memory of conflict and exclusion, . . . [but] also a memory of hope, a memory of freedom and resistance . . . In order for there to be resistance and the affirmation that is implied in the preservation of the memory of suffering, there must be an experience that includes some degree of liberation from the devaluation of human life by the dominant apparatuses of power/knowledge. Domination is not absolute as long as there is protest against it.[3]

[98]

The memories become dangerous when they are related to current situations of injustice. They are also dangerous in the sense that they challenge any complacency and cowardice amongst people of good will. Welch cites the poet Adrienne Rich's description of the challenge made to her thought by 'the raging stoic grandmothers' who demand that she does not simply buy into superficial liberation that affects some women but not others. 'The memories Rich carries are continually challenging. Her memories of oppression and resistance lead her to make choices, lead her to stand with the ordinary doers of extraordinary deeds.'[4]

Welch's reflections upon dangerous memories were inspired by Johann Baptist Metz, a liberation theologian, contemplating the situation in Latin America, who defined the task of Christian theology to be 'speaking about God by making the connection between the Christian message and the modern world visible and expressing the Christian tradition in this world as a dangerous memory'.[5] The essence of this dangerous memory for Metz is freedom, embodied in the paradigm of the Exodus and the life and teaching of Jesus. These memories are preserved among communities of resistance and solidarity. According to Welch, the concept of salvation is redefined in terms of solidarity, for it is in these communities and through the experience of solidarity that people find a voice, become conscious of their own oppression and begin to dream subversive dreams of liberation. The memories of oppression and resistance, when mixed together, spark and ignite a renewed fire of solidarity and resistance. People experience empowerment, a kind of power that is not like the power of oppression. It is a creative power that is not competitive or damaging to others but embracing, healing and uniting. It is a power experienced in specific locations where people learn through action, not afraid to make mistakes because they are not working with universal paradigms of truth. They may well be whistling in the wind of nihilism and despair, but they choose to risk acting as if this is not what reality is ultimately about. They choose an ethic of risk which is characterized by three elements 'each of which is essential to maintain resistance in the face of overwhelming odds: a redefinition of responsible action, grounding in community and strategic risk-taking'.[6] Responsible action consists of action that is creative, that makes it possible for further action to take place, that keeps a ball rolling towards a desired goal, even if that goal is out of sight and may remain so for ever. It is responsible because it is not done alone but in the context of community.

We do have the power to act alone to repress, to exploit, to blow up the world. We do not, however, have the power to make the world peaceful and just. That is a qualitatively different task and requires a qualitatively different exercise of power. Justice cannot be created for the poor by the rich, for it requires the transfer of power from the oppressors to the oppressed, the elimination of charity, and the enactment of justice.[7]

This is what differentiates theologies of liberation from European and North American liberal theology. Whereas liberal theology, represented by such people as Tillich, regards interdependence and what Tillich calls the 'contingency of our temporal and spatial being' as a threat to be overcome, feminist theologians and philosophers acknowledge, embrace and celebrate contingence,

our belonging to the web of life, as a complex, challenging, and wondrous gift . . . The dance of life, with all its contingence and ambiguity, can be good in itself . . . The 'beloved community' names the matrix within which life is celebrated, love is worshipped, and partial victories over injustice lay the groundwork for further acts of criticism and courageous defiance.[8]

Risk-taking is a communal enterprise and cannot be legislated for in advance but it is essential if the community is to be able to survive. However, Welch is clear that these communities are not communities of 'self-sacrifice'. The concept of self-sacrifice is inappropriate because it is generally a concept imposed by an outsider on people who may interpret their own actions rather in terms of integrity and community. What is lost in a community of resistance and solidarity is not the self: 'One may be deprived of the accoutrements of a successful self-wealth, prestige, and job security – but another self, one constituted by relationships with others, is found and maintained in acts of resistance.'[9] God for Welch is the completely immanent power of right-relationship, a 'presence that is both healing and fragile, constitutive of life and unambiguously present in the human condition . . . [but] absent in the atrocities of history and in humankind's despoliation of the earth'.[10] Elisabeth Schüssler Fiorenza has, of course, identified the communities of solidarity and resistance that women create as the *ekklesia* of women or women-church. Women are resident aliens in the structures of patriarchy; insiders and outsiders, they pitch their tent somewhere between the margins and the centre. It is possible to develop a theology of sainthood based upon the concepts of friendship and the *ekklesia* of women. The female saints form part of the dangerous memory of the *ekklesia* of women. The swish of their skirts whispers across the years and fans a spiritual wind that can energize those who struggle now. It is a friendship grounded in the sacred activity of remembrance. To remember is not simply to call to mind or to refuse to forget, it is to re-member, to reconstruct a life often broken and distorted by patriarchy, for the purpose of releasing its power into our lives. It is therefore a reciprocal relationship: the power that energizes and challenges us is the saints' gift to us; our reading of their lives from the perspective of a place of resistance to the patriarchy which has moulded their lives is our gift to them. Together we act to resist, to survive and to flourish.

Elisabeth Schüssler Fiorenza demonstrates this kind of friendship with her own patron saint St Elizabeth of Hungary. This is an interesting choice. Sharon Welch expressed some difficulty in identifying stories that 'empower me as someone who has a certain degree of privilege (as white, American, and middle class) . . . the memories that are constitutive of white, middle-class identity are hardly dangerous. They tend, rather, to reinforce the defence of privilege and often evoke despair or cynicism in the face of oppression.'[11] In Elizabeth of Hungary we have an example of a more than middle-class woman whose memory may be extremely dangerous and empowering for those of us who enjoy 'a certain degree of privilege'. It unquestionably is a dangerous and empowering memory in the manner in which Elisabeth Schüssler Fiorenza reconstitutes it. Elizabeth is usually portrayed as a thirteenth-century lady bountiful who against the wishes of the court and her in-laws went about doing good, founding hospitals and orphanages and, after her husband's death in the crusades, dedicated her life to God. Elisabeth Schüssler Fiorenza argues that hagiographical legend obscures the real Elizabeth who, like many late medieval women, desired, not be a lady bountiful, but a radical disciple who sought solidarity with the poor.

> What makes Elisabeth's life most outstanding, however is her sense of social justice. Elisabeth's contribution consisted in seeing poverty not as willed by God but as closely linked with the lifestyle of the rich and noble classes. She recognized that many consumer goods were unjustly taken away from the poor peasants who were her subjects, Peasants and petty workers paid for the luxurious living of the princes and lords. Not wanting to participate any more than necessary in such brutal exploitation, she vowed to eat only the food that had been justly acquired – a protest that anticipates by centuries our modern form of boycotting consumer goods in order to bring about change.[12]

She was deeply uncomfortable about relationships between mistresses and servants and would not allow herself to be addressed as 'mistress' or by the formal 'thou', but emphasized that her women companions were her friends and insisted that they should all address each other by the informal 'you'. It was this revolutionary praxis that angered those around her. Nothing challenges people's behaviour and political and economic systems like insiders opting out of them. Whilst he was alive her husband Ludwig supported her and protected her. Their love was real, but Elizabeth did not want to be completely absorbed by the relationship. When Ludwig died Elizabeth was told by her husband's family that she could only remain in her home if she gave up her revolutionary practices. She refused and had to flee with her children to live in a pigsty for a while. She eventually dedicated her life to Christ and, with money from a settlement from her family, built a hospice in which she served. But 'Elisabeth, who was spared the battering and brutality of a patriarchal marriage, was not spared that of the patriarchal church'.[13] The patriarchal church came to her in the shape of her confessor Conrad of Marburg who took over from a Franciscan in 1225. Conrad gained legal as well as spiritual control over Elizabeth's life and fortune. He aimed to break her will and force her into a conventional mode of religious life, in complete dependence upon him. He resorted to physical and emotional abuse to tame her will, and isolated her from her friends. Elizabeth responded by 'ostentatiously obeying him, yet astutely circumventing his injunctions in light of her own vocation and judgement',[14] comparing herself to a reed flattened by the waters of the flood which, when the water subsides, springs back up again as tall, erect and sublime as ever. She managed to resist Conrad's attempts to divert her from the path of radical discipleship which had been influenced by the Franciscan vision, although his brutal treatment of her led to her early death.

What is the nature of Elizabeth's friendship with twentieth-century women, what energy is realized from re-membering her from the distortions of hagiography?

> Despite its medieval flavour Elisabeth's vision of radical discipleship resonates with Catholic women today who understand themselves as fully committed and responsible Christians. The historical image of Elisabeth, freed from its legendary trappings and rescued from its medieval limitations, does not restrict women's vision and self-understanding to family, children and feminine behaviour appropriate to the 'white lady'. Instead, this image encourages women to break out of the cultural and religious limitations of femininity to a self-image and

identity of full personhood and radical discipleship. Moreover, such an ideal suggests that women's struggles for liberation must not be limited to the values and interests of middle-class women. Rather, these struggles must work to build a new sisterhood of discipleship – one that transcends sex-stereotyped roles, social class, and religious caste as well as our separation in time and space.[15]

So Elizabeth's voice and life echo down the centuries, encouraging us to break out from the moulds of femininity within which our culture seeks to confine us, to resist in fact all the social stratifications which keep us apart from one another and which prevent solidarity among women. Her story also counsels us to expect resistance, often violent, when we do seek to follow radical vocations, but to never give up on that vocation, bending like a reed when necessary. Elizabeth can most certainly be claimed as part of a community of solidarity and resistance. Her memory empowers and challenges us, comforts and disturbs us. She also demonstrates what Welch has to say about love in communities of resistance: 'Resistance to oppression is often based on a love that transcends the limits of social systems, a love that leads us to value ourselves more, and leads us to hope for more than the established cultural system is willing to grant.'[16] It is a love that is grounded in self-love, even though Christian discourse has generally excluded the recognition of this fact. In choosing to follow her vocation against raging opposition from Church and state/family Elizabeth demonstrated confidence in herself and self-love. Hence her actions did not involve self-sacrifice as such but self-affirmation that involved the letting go of much of her privilege. She operated according to a vision of love, which, in Welch's description of the black poet June Jordan,

> is both self-affirming and affirming of others, a love that denounces injustice, heals the wounds of exploitation, and builds a community of strong individuals . . . Middle-class people can sustain work for justice when empowered by love for those who are oppressed. Such love is far more energizing than guilt, duty or self-sacrifice. Love for others leads us to accept accountability (in contrast to feeling guilt) and motivates our search for ways to end our complicity with structures of oppression.[17]

We recognize Elizabeth as friend, but she cannot be simply adopted as sister – there are differences between her and twentieth-century Hungarian women. She was a medieval royal woman who lived in a world totally different from the world that any woman in the twentieth century occupies. She therefore reminds us of our differences from each other and challenges us to build up our *ekklesia* on the basis of solidarity that acknowledges and embraces difference, whilst working to overcome structural inequality.

Communities of resistance need to contain within them the memories of those who have gone before. We need ancestral guardians, friends from the past, whose lives were lived against the grain of patriarchy but also against the grain of our own lives, who help us to remember with gratitude that others went before us risking and resisting within their own particular cultural context, pushing the ball closer to the goal, passing it on to us to push a bit further on to those who will find our cultural conditioning as alienating as we do the medieval period. They also challenge us to recognize that behaviour which twentieth-century feminists may dismiss as based upon destructive patriarchal notions of 'self-sacrifice' (e.g. severe fasting) was in fact a means of resistance and solidarity within a particular cultural context. The medieval woman saints Angela of Foligno and Elizabeth of Ruete, who fasted for twelve and fifteen years respectively, were exercising control over the arena in which women did have power – food. They were exercising their radical discipleship at the heart of the construction of womanhood in their society and they were resisting it. Women gave up that which they had control over, just as men in search of a radical vocation gave up their property and money.[18] But fasting was also a political act. In refusing to care about food women rejected what society believed was their 'natural' vocation; in refusing to take part in the communal family meal, the woman dissociated herself from the ties and obligations of kinship. In rejecting those things which their society valued most – food and good health – women acted as a counter sign to the values of that society. Severe fasting also brought with it visions – direct encounters with the divine which gave the women who received them a certain amount of autonomy from the structures and strictures of the Church.[19] Friendship involves recognizing the different cultural contexts in which we work, and recognizing that women may have chosen practices which we now regard as sickening and destructive as positive actions of resistance.

One of the problems with hagiography which has already been noted is the tendency to turn its subjects into lonesome heroes, isolated from any community. However this is less pronounced in the lives of women than of men. Even Elizabeth of Hungary, who may at first sight appear to plough a lone furrow, was first of all influenced by the praxis of Sts Francis and Clare, and her personal vocation came during a time when women all over Europe were seeking ways to engage in active Christian ministry in the world. She did not work alone but first relied on her husband's support, encouragement and protection. She always ministered along with female companions and eventually founded a community. Women saints were part of communities of resistance then, just as now they form part of contemporary communities of defiance.

David Matthew Matzko in his reflections upon sainthood from a post-modern perspective argues that saints are a scandal to modernity because they escape all definition. It is impossible to define a saint:

> Sometimes a saint is bold and confident; sometimes saints are meek. Sometimes a saint is a person who represents an ideal pattern of behaviour; at other times the saint creates an ideal through living in an unprecedented way, a way that is unexpected yet recognised by others to be good, courageous, compassionate, humble, holy, moral or miraculous, and the list goes on.[20]

Matzko goes on to argue that saints cannot be saintly as individuals. They are constituted by others: 'saints represent aspirations for human life, they mediate God's presence, they overcome barriers and create human community in such ways that cannot be explained – only retold. The saints are a scandal to modernity when they create possibilities for human community through the particularity of a people.'[21] Community is therefore at the heart of sainthood and the aspect of sainthood that makes it 'a scandal to modern universalism, rationality, democracy, and immanence'. Matzko goes on to illustrate his point with reference to a woman who is not an officially canonized saint but who, as we have seen, is regarded as a people's saint in some parts of the world – Dorothy Day:

> She cannot be called the founder of the Catholic Worker movement insofar as the movement is not an organisation, but she is its matriarch. Calling her mother rather than founder locates Day in a network of continuing relationships. She is matriarch because there is a continuing line of mothers, fathers, brothers and sisters to carry on the movement and her memory. Her memory holds together a disparate collection of people who always lean on the border of being in or out of what it means to remember her. Dorothy Day's saintliness depends on how well these folk can remember her and pray. Her memory is her Catholic spirituality, her hospitality, her pacifism, her deeds of love, and her cry for justice. For those who remember her she is a saint. She is a saint who, like Ignatius of Loyola, was dedicated to remembering, venerating, and following the saints.[22]

And the story is even more complex than Matzko acknowledges, because it is very obvious that Day was not a lonesome hero. She always worked with others and was well knitted into a web of relationships throughout her life and work.

The lives of the saints form part of the dangerous memory of Christianity and the lives of the women saints form part of the dangerous memory of women defying the patriarchal construction of Christianity. They form what Foucault identified as a 'subjugated discourse', which arises in contradistinction to the dominant discourse. That memory is inspiring, encouraging, challenging and demanding. The women saints are our friends in as much as in the memory of their lives and work women find the resources, the strength, the encouragement, the *jouissance* or passion to continue to build *ekklesia* and we are their friends in as much as we re-member them with women's hands and through women's eyes.

Remembering is a sacred activity, it always has been for Christians. Indeed, Christianity is founded upon the command to remember. Augustine believed that God was found through the memory. Charles Wesley once described the Holy Spirit as the 'Remembrancer Divine' because it is in the remembering, in the refusing to forget, that we defy the forces of our world that seek to deconstruct, to cover, to 'lose' those who represent justice because they are either martyrs for it or victims of injustice. Remembering, to use a famous phrase, keeps 'the rumour of God alive' or rather the rumour of God's vision, God's reign, God's beloved community, alive and therefore a dangerous possibility. Rowan Williams has identified two reasons why people should remember the dead: first because they need to know and remember that the world we live in 'is a world *shared* with others they cannot fully know, and *made* by others'[23] and this determines to a great extent what we can and cannot do with it. Second, we need to remember that we have been 'bought at a price', not just the 'price we enjoy celebrating – the generosity of benefactors, the self-sacrifice of heroes; but the fact we are, willy-nilly, the heirs of a process of violence and pain, power built on the back of suffering'.[24] This is a situation we need to understand and not just seek vindication for, in order to be better able to identify today's victims. In doing so we learn to 'remember for the future'. For Christian feminists though, an essential part of 'remembering for the future' involves remembering not only the suffering and pain but also the joy and the defiance of destructive forces. As Mary Grey has noted, memory can only be truly empowering when it is based on something other than humiliation.[25]

This interpretation of sainthood is somewhat close to that offered by Karl Rahner in his *Theological Investigations*. Rahner does not, of course, use the language of friendship and he writes about the saints in the language of the heroic. Canonized saints 'tower over all other "saints" – in other words, over us ordinary Christians – by their "heroic" virtue'.[26] In proclaiming a saint the Church proves herself to be what she professes to be – holy. But there is something in his theology of sainthood that resonates with this particular feminist interpretation:

> They are the initiators and the creative models of the holiness which happens to be right for, and is the task of, their particular age. They create a new style; they prove that a certain form of life and activity is a really genuine possibility: they show . . . that one can be a Christian even in this way; they make such a type of person believable as a Christian type. Their significance begins therefore not merely after they are dead. Their death is rather the seal put upon their task of being creative models, a task which they had in the Church during their lifetime, and their living-on means that the example they have given remains in the Church in a permanent form.[27]

In the saints then we have 'creative models' of what it means to be a Christian in specific contexts. For Rahner it is important that the saints are so different from one another and that they take that difference up into their sanctity, for it is vital that sanctity is not merely an abstract or uniform context but is understood to be truly incarnational, possible in every age and circumstance and amongst a variety of different people. Otherwise 'ordinary' Christians would not regard sanctity as part of their concern. A similar approach is adopted by David Matzko in his doctoral dissertation, but he has a much stronger sense of the communitarian nature of sainthood:

> For Christian theology, sainthood and the memory of naming particular saints are intelligible only when set within a network of relationships, a common memory, and a history of interpretative practice, all of which make God present to the world. I propose that saints are the inhabitants of this common memory and network of relationships, and I make the stronger assertion that 'naming saints' is the means by which this common life is created. I assert not only that saints are a *means* of naming a continuous history of God's presence to the world but also that they *are* this continuing presence.[28]

For Rahner and Matzko then, as for feminists who might adopt this minimalist approach to sainthood, the primary value of the saints lies in their role as encouraging, challenging models of, in Rahner's language, 'holiness' (feminists would probably prefer 'wholeness' or 'subversive female presence'). They are incarnations of the divine presence in every age and circumstance. They are the memory through which we interpret ourselves and our world. Our relationship with them is the relationship of the quilt-makers to those who preserve the quilts today and it is deep, meaningful and, indeed, essential for the building of 'beloved communities' or *ekklesia*.

But for many women this theology of sainthood does not adequately account for their relationship with the saints. Ironically, their relationship with the saints fits more comfortably in an 'orthodox' approach. Many people's relationship to the saints is close to that set out by the bishops of Vatican II, who also developed a theology of sacramental remembering when reflecting upon the saints, but who went further than this:

> Exactly as Christian communion between men [*sic*] on their earthly pilgrimage brings us closer to Christ, so our community with the saints joins us to Christ . . . It is most fitting, therefore, that we love those friends and co-heirs of Jesus Christ who are also our brothers [*sic*] and outstanding benefactors, and that we give due thanks to God for them, 'humbly invoking them, and having recourse to their prayers, their aid and help' . . . we seek from the saints 'example in their way of life, fellowship in their communion, and the help of their intercession'.[29]

For a Christian feminist this description may beg a whole set of difficult questions which we will explore shortly, but it does speak about the relationship between saint and friend in a manner that captures the reality of the *relationship* in a way that 'mere' remembrance fails to do. Joan of Arc's relationship with her saints is not accounted for by simply a calling to remembrance, neither is Thérèse of Lisieux's relationship with her friends Sts Agnes and Cecilia, although remembering is certainly an aspect of that friendship. Theirs was a relationship with people who lived in the past but also existed in a real and tangible way in the present and with whom they could engage in some sort of meaningful and mutual dialogue. This is a relationship which many women still experience today. Carter Heyward in a sermon preached on All Saints' Day 1983 described our relationship to the saints in these terms:

> To remember is to put back together that which has been dismembered, torn violently into pieces on the basis of fear, greed, hatred, competition, and denial. To remember those whose lives, bodies,

spirits, and hearts have been broken is to call them and bring them, by the power of the One whose name is Love, into solidarity with us. We stand with them bonded by God, as lovers and workers together in this world on behalf of one another, ourselves and the Holy Spirit . . . I believe in heaven. I believe that those who have died are with us now. I have come to believe that the place to find and get in touch with these saints is wherever we are right now, at every moment of our lives here on this earth.[30]

And in a later reflection upon theological lessons she had learned from Nicaragua, taking as her text the strident cry of Mother Jones (1830–1930), an American of Irish descent, a powerful and subversive force in labour relations, who urged people to 'pray for the dead and fight like hell for the living', Heyward comments that the first lesson to learn is that the living includes those who are dead:

Faithful people assume that women, men, and children who have died defending the Nicaraguan revolution against the United States-sponsored *contras* are not dead at all but rather continue to participate in the struggle against *imperialismo*. At the funerals of those killed by *contras*, when the people respond, '*Presente!*' as each name is read, they are not merely asking that those who have died stay with them. They are announcing that those who have died now live. They are proclaiming that those whose bodies are being laid to rest have not gone at all but rather are *presente!*, stronger than ever as a force to be reckoned with, members of a Body that cannot be buried and forgotten.[31]

This she believes is related to the Nicaraguan insight that breathing bodies are not necessarily alive. Death cannot separate someone from the body but breathing does not necessarily make one part of it – a great many people are spiritually dead. Heyward is convinced that this faith springs not primarily from 'the teaching of the Church' but from the Nicaraguans' experience of having 'lived among the living rather than the dead'.[32] And this is why it is foreign to most Westerners. We live in the realm of the dead, we are taught how to stay dead by grasping for power but

never to thirst after justice
never to hunger with the poor
never to celebrate what we hold in common
never to live among the living
never to live![33]

To live is to know solidarity as part of a 'beloved community' and it is that sense of solidarity that lies behind the Nicaraguans' faith in the

living of their dead. It must be possible to offer a feminist theological
account of this faith, for it is part of the feminist agenda to take
seriously the experience of those at the 'base' and to recognize that
the liberal agenda excludes a great deal of 'wisdom', particularly
women's wisdom and the wisdom of the non-white and the non-
middle class. However difficult, galling or frightening it may be for
a Christian feminist to approach questions of life after death, the
feminist project and the principles upon which it is based require,
even demand, that we do so. We have to make some 'women-sense'
of what to many women, past and present, has been an essential,
life-giving, life-saving relationship.

A daring theology of sainthood

I believe that it is possible, very tentatively but very daringly, to work
towards a feminist theology of sainthood which takes account of the
experience of friendship between women and saints as outlined
above, by drawing upon and weaving together some central tenets in
feminist theology.

THE BODY OF CHRISTA/SOPHIA

We have already noted the problem that feminist theology has with
heroes of any sort. Taking any individual, disassociating him or her
from the masses, ascribing unique qualities to them and then making
the masses dependent upon the hero for some kind of salvation is a
fundamentally patriarchal model, emphasizing distance and detach-
ment and hierarchy between people. Women, it has been argued by
people such as Carol Gilligan, see value in and draw strength from a
sense of connection, of horizontal relating, from solidarity.[34] This has
led feminist theologians to take a long hard look at christology and to
attempt to re-image the doctrine of Christ in such a way as to rid it
of its patriarchal hero basis. Among the most successful attempts to
redeem christology from patriarchy is that of Rita Nakashima Brock.
Pulling the rug out from under all hero christologies, she points out
that women's experience teaches us that 'if Jesus is reported to have
been capable of profound love and concern for others, he was first
loved and respected by the concrete persons of his life. If he was
liberated, he was involved in a community of mutual liberation.'[35]
The Gospels themselves give us hints of this: Jesus relies heavily
on his friends for hospitality, he never travels alone, his mission is to

establish a new community which subverts all previous notions of kinship and is based purely upon friendship. This vision grows as he encounters people who challenge his theology – see, for example, his encounter with the Syro-Phoenician woman (Mark 7.24–30). For Brock, Jesus *participates* in what she calls 'Christa/Community' which is 'erotic power', or passion, the power of right-relationship. 'Jesus participates centrally in this Christa/Community, but he neither brings erotic power into being nor controls it. He is brought into being through it and participates in the cocreation of it . . . He neither reveals it nor embodies it, but he participates in its revelation and embodiment.'[36] The term 'Christa' was the title given to a female figure placed upon a crucifix created by Edwina Sandys and displayed in the Cathedral of St John the Divine, New York, until the controversy it caused prompted the bishop to have it taken down. Brock uses the term to shift the focus of salvation off the lone heroic figure of Jesus. To detach Jesus from the web of relationships that formed him is to do violence both to him and to those pushed into the background.

Carter Heyward, in a discussion about what it means to be 'in Christ', makes much of Jesus' rejection of the mantle of prophet in Mark 8.27–29: ' "Prophet" means God will act *in the future*; "Christ" means God is acting *now*. Prophets speak of what God will do farther down the road; Christ makes things happen in human life immediately, here and now. Prophets say that God is coming; Christ means God is here.'[37] Thus Christ is the presence of God in the world and to be 'in Christ' is to be in touch with our *dunamis*, 'raw, spontaneous power, unable to be controlled, boxed in, or possessed as our own; *able only to be shared* and, in so being, to re-create the world'.[38] It is a power that is released when people strive towards right-relationship, it is to love with passion, it is to realize our power to make a difference in the minutiae of our lives, it is to incarnate God's 'Yes' to justice and 'No' to violence and destruction. Heyward later identifies that power as Christa.[39] In particular Christa is manifest among the outcast and despised women with whom the rest of us are called to stand in solidarity; this is how we become and manifest the body of Christa. Christa is often most clearly manifest in and to women when they share their stories, in which they hear each other's pain and find the strength to resist.

The concept of the body of Christ is at the heart of the 'orthodox' understanding of sainthood. The *koinonia*, the communion enjoyed by members of the body of Christ (i.e. the Church) cannot be broken by death: 'The members of Christ's body mutually serve one another in building up the whole in unity. Since power goes out from the saints their merits and virtues may be said to constitute, metaphorically speaking, a treasure.'[40] It is in the nature of the communion enjoyed by members of the body of Christ that Christians live with and for one another. Whereas orthodox theology traces this communion back to the heroic figure of Jesus, feminists such as Brock believe that Jesus himself was the product of such communion. In the body of Christa/Community all are intricately and intimately related to one another, interdependent in such a way that there is a spontaneous mutual exchange of gifts. So one person's actions can benefit another – this is a concept with which modern Western society with its rampant individualism has real difficulties, but not feminism. The whole feminist project is built upon mutual empowerment, dependence upon a mutual exchange of positive energy and action for justice for the purpose of forming, maintaining and developing true community/ *koinonia* based upon solidarity and mutuality. This was also an idea dear to the heart of Dietrich Bonhoeffer, whose reflections upon community led him to assert in language which in many ways grated against his Protestant tradition that being 'in Christ' means that one person's merits are no longer their own but belong to the whole Christian community.[41] The difficulty as far as Christian feminism is concerned (and I am sure that this is a difficulty shared with others) is in accounting for the experience of mutual exchange of gifts with the dead in a more concrete manner than simply through sacramental remembrance, although many Christian feminists would not seek to go beyond the concept of sacramental remembrance.

Before going any further it is essential to recognize the difficulties many (including some Christian feminists) have with the term (but not the concept) of Christa. It could be argued that the term Christa does not conjure up images of community but simply a representation of another individual – a female Christ. Since both the concept of the Christa and the body of Christ are meant to convey the same thing, the presence in embodied community of the divine, it might be more helpful to speak of Sophia. Sophia, or *Hochma* in Hebrew, is Wisdom, a personified attribute of God in Israel's wisdom tradition. She (for wisdom is personified as female) is immanent in creation, the presence of God moving through history binding people into friendship with God and each other. This is why Grey offered the Sophia myth as one that conveys revelation through connection. I will use Sophia from now on when speaking about the presence of God in community. This avoids both the identification of Christ-ness solely with Jesus (Christian theologians down the centuries have identified Jesus as the incarnation of Sophia) and the ambiguity of the term Christa, but is still true to both the 'orthodox' and the feminist use of their respective terms, for it conveys the continual incarnation of the divine in human community.

Carter Heyward may point us in a fruitful direction when reflecting upon her experience in Nicaragua. Heyward notes that the second lesson she learned from her *compañeras/os* there was that the Body (of Sophia) is flesh and blood and bone that needs attention: 'For Nicaragua's revolutionary Christians, the Body of Christ is actively whatever Body – person or group – is struggling against unjust suffering . . . While the Body of Christ is broken in every act of violence, greed, or bigotry, it is rising in every act of solidarity with those who are oppressed, whatever their credo, colour or culture.'[42] To be fully human is to live as part of the Body, to recognize inter-dependence and to live in it, to live and work for the common good. It is in solidarity that Sophia is realized, incarnated and, very significantly for our purposes, 'Those who live for the living are the Body that cannot be killed. They are the holiest of sacraments. When we stand together, we are they. This is embodiment, and it is the incarnation of God.'[43] So those who have died are re-embodied in those who live in solidarity. How?

To answer this I think it will be helpful to weave into the Sophia pattern two more feminist concepts: Rosemary Radford Ruether's reflections upon death and Grace Jantzen's reflections upon a new model of soteriology.

Jantzen has noted that in the Hebrew Scriptures God's will for humanity is often talked about in terms of flourishing (see, for example, Proverbs 11.28; 14.11; and Psalms 37.36, 92.12 and 103.17), a specific image which is virtually absent from the New Testament, although analogous language of fullness and abundance is used. As a metaphor it has received hardly any attention from theologians ancient or modern, although theologians of liberation are now reclaiming it. Jantzen believes 'that the contrast between salvation and flourishing is a gendered contrast'.[44] Whereas the metaphor of flourishing sug-gests abundance, energy, and movement from strength to strength that is self-sufficient, salvation (which is also, of course, a metaphor, even though it is rarely recognized as such) suggests the need for rescue by someone, for outside intervention. One takes an optimistic view of the human state, the other a pessimistic. One assumes interconnectedness ('flourishing is impossible by oneself alone'[45]) and is aware of the dynamics of flourishing ('who suffers that I may flourish?'), the other is individualistic and depoliticized. One is concerned with this world and the embodied beings within it, the other is concerned with the next world and the souls that may get into it: 'The interconnections between the construction of masculinity and the socio-economic system of competitive individualism have received much attention. What has been less frequently noted is how neatly it coheres with a theology built on the model of personal salvation.'[46] Jantzen draws upon Luce Irigaray's observation that patriarchy has always been fixated on other worlds, thus distracting itself from this world and our responsibilities in it and to it. Women are identified with despised and distrusted matter and men with the 'pure' realm of spirit. The metaphor of flourishing is therefore part of the subjugated knowledge of women's spirituality, resurrecting and insurrecting itself against male-constructed notions of 'salvation'. It is an image which is to be found in some form in the writings of Hildegard of Bingen who employs the language of horticulture in her theology. For example a hymn to Mary employs a variety of flourishing metaphors:

> Hail to you, O greenest, most fertile branch!
> You budded forth amidst breezes and winds . . .
> In you, the most stunning flower has blossomed
> and gives off its sweet odor to all the herbs and roots,
> which were dry and thirsting before your arrival.
> Now they spring forth in fullest green! . . .
> And, because of you, nourishment is given to the human
>   family.[47]

Rosemary Radford Ruether, in her reflections as an ecofeminist, regards the belief in an immortal soul and the overwhelming desire to live for ever to be both a symptom and a contributing factor towards our sense of disconnection from our earth which has led to its exploitation and destruction. She believes that we need to embrace the fact that, just as 'the sustaining of organic community of plant and animal life is a continual cycle of growth and decay', so it must be in the case of community:

> By pretending that we can immortalize ourselves, our souls, and perhaps even our bodies for some future resurrection, we are immortalizing our garbage and polluting the earth, If we are really to learn to recycle our garbage as fertilizer for new growth, our waste as matter for new artifacts, we need a spirituality of recycling that

accepts ourselves as part of that process of growth, decay, reintegration into the earth and new growth.[48]

Human bodies, like all matter, decay and are 'composted back into the nexus of matter to rise again as new organic forms'.[49] And Ruether believes the same must hold true for human consciousness or souls, but 'perhaps we might think of a great consciousness underlying the whole life process that carries and expands with the remembering of each of our small selves, while letting go of the illusion of immortal self within each of our many mortal embodiments'.[50] Our selves are taken back into the earth which, as feminist theologians such as Sallie McFague and Jantzen have suggested, can be imaged as God's body, a metaphor which is panentheistic, i.e. 'a view of the God–world relationship in which all things have their origins in God and nothing exists outside God, though this does not mean that God is reduced to these things'.[51] Taken into God they become compost, nourishing future generations, aiding them to flourish if they use the legacy wisely. As Ruether suggests, our consciousness or souls (or whatever label you want to apply to that mysterious aspect of beings that cannot be explained merely physically, although feminists and all anti-dualists would want to emphasize that there can be no disconnection between the body and this mysterious element) must be also taken into the earth/body of God where it too, along with and as part of our embodied existence, becomes part of the compost. In this sense we do not fall from life into nothingness but from one form of life into another. Any gardener knows that the compost bin is not a tomb, but is full of life and energy. One might also speculate that those who have been most 'alive' in Heyward's sense of that word in this life add a particular richness to the compost, although all ultimately play their part. Using this model, the Nicaraguan belief, that those who had been part of the 'beloved community', but had died, still live, becomes even more attractive and comprehensible. Those who have died continue to nourish and sustain their community from the heart of the body of God which has received them. Their energy, their thirst for justice warms and nourishes the roots of their community, like compost around a plant. As I understand it, modern science now believes that there is no dualism between matter and energy but that all is energy – what may look solid 'dead matter' is in reality a dance of energy, so in talking about energy I am not falling into a dualistic mind-set.

It is easy to apply this metaphor to the experience of the saints: a community may feel particularly empowered, nourished and enabled to flourish by the energy of a particular person or persons who represent to them a particular form of creative and empowering energy which was shared by many, just as Jesus came to represent the energy of the communities which formed him and in which he moved and lived. He represented their experience of being embodied divinity, of feeling the energy of God between them in their struggles and joy. This energy they recognized in figures from their community's past, the patriarchs and prophets, but also knew to be manifest differently in their own time and context. The apostles (including Mary Magdalen) and other New Testament figures also came to represent this energy. It must be possible to recognize this without lapsing into hero worship or dependency. St Joan tapped into the creative energy of the community of virgin saints represented by Sts Katherine and Margaret, whose defiance and resistance energized her. St Thérèse of Lisieux similarly was filled with the energy of Sts Agnes and Cecilia, an energy she felt when visiting their tombs. Perhaps this helps to make some sense or a different sense out of why people feel the need to visit the burial sites of saints and to touch their relics. In doing so people recognize, at least at a subconscious level, the integration of the human person: bodies and souls/consciousness/energy cannot be separated. A particular place in which a saint's body was laid to rest becomes a sacramental focus for their energy, and so people engage in what Alphonse Dupront has called *une thérapie par l'espace* (therapy of distance).[52] They recognize that their immediate environment does not provide them with the energy they need and so they set off on a journey (which for Dupront symbolized needs unsatisfied) to find the right energy. Although this energy, having been absorbed into the greater consciousness which is God, can be tapped into in any place, there is a special sacramental dimension to some places, just as there are special sacramental dimensions to some people. All people and all places are potential sacraments of God's presence but some, through the consensus of a community or communities, become symbolic focuses for divine energy which is constantly being expanded, enhanced and changed by the embodied consciousness of those who are taken into it. God is not a static closed being but is relationship (this is at least hinted at in the doctrine of the Trinity), and being in relationship means being open to being changed by it.

This theology may be enough for some, but it still does not explain how it is that many women and men feel themselves to have a personal relationship with saints with strong personalities and bodies. One possible explanation is offered by Rita Nakashima Brock, who interprets the disciples' experience of the resurrection of Jesus as 'evidence of the presence of the magic of play space'.[53] This is the space where the imagination roams free, where dreams seemingly impossible in a patriarchally constructed society are dreamt, and dualisms overcome; it is a place in which Sophia thrives. The community of which Jesus was a part refused to allow death to defeat them or him: 'Despite the brutalness of death under oppression, the community of faithful disciples restores erotic power and the hope of wholeness for the community by not letting go of their relationships to each other and not letting Jesus' death be the end of their community.'[54] Brock believes that regardless of their status as events in history, these magical, playful experiences can heal and transform; they are part of the experience of Sophia, and she relates her own experience of seeing and feeling her dead mother and those of other women in which interestingly there is a physical dimension and a sense of absorption:

> Spent from anger and grief, I lay quietly on the floor, eyes open. I felt, more than heard, a wind at the open doorway to the hall and saw my mother, whole and healed, float into the room toward me. Parallel to my body and several feet above it, she looked into my eyes and said, 'It's all right.' Her toes touched mine and she entered my body through my feet. I felt a euphoric, peaceful energy return to me. I knew I was going to be all right after that, and I have been.[55]

Modern science tends to relegate such experiences simply to the level of psychological delusion, a symptom of grief or illness or depression, but a feminist theology cannot quite so easily dismiss experiences which appear to transcend and rend asunder the dictates of scientific dualism. Instead these experiences are taken up into a tapestry of myth that we weave over our lives, using the language that patriarchy hates, the language of symbol, image and metaphor, imprecise and unscientific, to bind us in the common project of making sense out of the world in which we live. One of the recent developments in feminist theology has been reflection upon space, space as patriarchally ordered and the creation of women-space.[56] The space of play, of imagination, of magic has been denigrated, squeezed out and often demonized under patriarchal systems; it has become the realm of the sick, the feckless, the lazy, the dangerous and, of course, of women. So too, incidentally, has relationship with the dead. Despite its ancient belief in the Communion of Saints, orthodox Christianity has forbidden any kind of communication with the dead (except the saints) – an activity which in Western culture, at least, is associated specifically with women. There are good reasons for condemning those who seek to claim that communication with the dead takes place in a realm outside of play and imagination, and therefore believe that the dead are as exploitable and manipulable as the living. But in the place of the imagination communication with the dead such as experienced by Brock can be healing.

The space of the imagination is the space of resistance and defiance, a space to imagine life as it could be, a world transformed. This is why imaginative and playful pursuits like art, drama, dance, story-telling and so on flourish on the margins of society. Feminist theologians like Brock seek to reclaim the space of play, imagination and magic from the denigration of patriarchy and hold it up as a space of importance and value, an essential space in the building of 'beloved community' or *ekklesia*. To say that someone is imagining something is therefore most certainly *not* to say that what they are doing is not 'real' or not 'true' or is self-deluding, but that they are engaging in an activity necessary for healing and survival in the context in which they move. To imagine is to transcend all the false limitations placed upon our experience by patriarchy, it is to walk through the walls which the straight patriarchal mind erects around us, creating false and dangerous divisions of space. In engaging in personal friendships with saints women are using the space of imagination and play. In that place the embodied energy of women and men can be remembered, just as Brock remembered her mother and the disciples Jesus.

Such experiences may not be consciously sought, they are inevitably deeply mysterious, but they are always a powerful experience of passion or what Brock would call erotic power, the power of mutuality and solidarity. We might draw upon the notion of the sacramental again. The divine may with our co-operation focus its energy in a variety of different ways at different times. She may then choose to incarnate herself in the lives of some in the re-embodiment of a particular person who had long since been absorbed back into her being. She can re-summon, reknit their embodied energy, energy which has been changed, expanded and enriched by others, and come to us in the form of the saints with whom we can bond and enjoy a real, living friendship as individuals and as communities. These friendships, born in the sacred space of the imagination where walls can be walked through (note how this activity figures in the resurrection stories of Jesus: Luke 24.36; John 20.19), become places for nourishing and flourishing, for resistance and solidarity. Through these friendships we access God and therefore the energies of all who have gone before us, the 'great cloud of witnesses'. If feminist theology is right and God is experienced primarily through the reality of relationships, the saints provide us with one particular type of relational route to the divine as communities and as individuals.

A daring theology of sainthood has emerged which, by weaving together some of the themes from recent feminist theology, has created a tapestry of theology which, I think, avoids the pitfalls of dualism whilst being true to the real lived experience of many women. The lives of the women labelled saints (and indeed all women) are taken into the body of God where they are not absorbed or neutralized in some kind of cosmic soup but become part of the divine energy nurturing our world and our lives and providing us with the energy necessary to flourish, to embody Sophia. Yet in the space of imagination and play individuals can be summoned. We can cry *Presente!* to saints with whom we identify, who represent to us and our communities the energy we need, and in the space of the imagination the divine energy refashions herself in a specific embodied person with whom we can communicate.

Of course, one of the walls that women have and will continue to walk through regarding saints is the official canon of saints. Communities have always venerated people as saints without official church approval and ignored some of those whom the Church has approved. As the Durham quilt testifies, women are certainly prepared to name women as sacramental friends who stood or stand no chance of making it into the official canon. Women as women-church claim the right and authority to name their own reality, to name those whom male-church ignores. In recognizing that there are many saints unknown to the Church, the fathers have no real grounds for objection when women claim their right as Church, as part of the body of Sophia, to name their beloved dead. In holding up women who are not official saints, women not only draw attention to the non-patriarchal rich diversity of the divine consciousness and body which sustains us all, but also serve to de-heroize the concept of sainthood. They also draw attention to the injustices perpetrated upon women by male-church and seek to right them. In remembering and celebrating the lives of the nine million women wiped off the face of the earth during the medieval witch hunts, which were themselves then erased from church history, women demand that the Church acknowledge both the crime and the fear of women's wisdom and power that drove it to commit such unspeakable evil. They draw attention to the reversal in which patriarchy often engages: good is labelled evil and injustice holy. In celebrating women as godly whom others labelled evil and devilish women walk through the walls of patriarchal reality and reveal them to be as flimsy as tissue.

We are all part of the same project – building up friendship, community and solidarity. In that sense all those who are involved in the struggle for justice are 'saints'; we are all seeking to incarnate the divine in our midst. Any one of us and every one of us could become sacramental symbols and friends of the struggle. One practice that has become popular in feminist circles in recent years is the women's picnic or dinner. Women come together to eat and each creates a placemat or brings an object which represents a woman who has had a particularly nourishing role in her life. In Christian feminist circles grandmothers, mothers, aunts, sisters, lovers, friends, teachers rub shoulders with writers, artists, philosophers, theologians and official saints. Any and every one can make it onto a woman's placemat or a quilt, perhaps the Christian feminist equivalents of the medieval rood screens. And all of us 'in Sophia' will also be in those who are chosen as sacramental symbols and friends. What Rita Nakashima Brock says about Jesus can also be said about those we designate or treat as saints:

> Jesus is like the whitecap on a wave. The whitecap is momentarily set off from the swell that is pushing it up, making us notice it. But the visibility of the whitecap, which draws our attention, rests on the enormous pushing power of the sea – of its power to push with life-giving labour, to buoy up all lives, and to unite diverse shores with its restless energy. That sea becomes monstrous and chaotically destructive when we try to control it, and its life-giving power is denied. Jesus' power lies with the great swells of the ocean without which the white foam is not brought to visibility.[5]

NOTES

1 Sharon Welch, *A Feminist Ethic of Risk* (Minneapolis: Fortress Press, 1990).
2 Welch, *A Feminist Ethic of Risk*, p. 133.
3 Sharon Welch, *Communities of Resistance and Solidarity: A Feminist Theology of Liberation* (Maryknoll: Orbis Books, 1985), p. 39.
4 Welch, *A Feminist Ethic of Risk*, p. 154.
5 Johann Baptist Metz, *Faith in History and Society: Toward a Practical Fundamentalist Society* (New York: Seabury Press, 1980), p. 89.

6 Welch, *A Feminist Ethic of Risk*, p. 20.
7 Welch, *A Feminist Ethic of Risk*, p. 51.
8 Welch, *A Feminist Ethic of Risk*, pp. 160–1.
9 Welch, *A Feminist Ethic of Risk*, p. 165.
10 Welch, *A Feminist Ethic of Risk*, p. 177.
11 Welch, *A Feminist Ethic of Risk*, pp. 155–6.
12 Elisabeth Schüssler Fiorenza, *Discipleship of Equals: A Critical Feminist Ekklesia-logy of Liberation* (London: SCM, 1993), p. 45.
13 Schüssler Fiorenza, *Discipleship of Equals*, p. 46.
14 Schüssler Fiorenza, *Discipleship of Equals*, p. 46.
15 Schüssler Fiorenza, *Discipleship of Equals*, p. 47.
16 Welch, *A Feminist Ethic of Risk*, p. 161.
17 Welch, *A Feminist Ethic of Risk*, p. 162.
18 Caroline Bynum, *Holy Feast and Holy Fast: The Religious Significance of Food to Medieval Women* (Berkeley: University of California Press, 1987).
19 Walter Vandereychen and Ron van Deth, *From Fasting Saints to Anorexic Girls: The History of Self-Starvation* (London: Athlone Press, 1994); Rudolph M. Bell, *Holy Anorexia* (Chicago: University of Chicago Press, 1985).
20 David Matthew Matzko, 'Postmodernism, saints and scoundrels', *Modern Theology*, vol. 9, no. 1 (January 1993), p. 30.
21 Matzko, 'Postmodernism, saints and scoundrels', p. 30.
22 Matzko, 'Postmodernism, saints and scoundrels', pp. 30–1.
23 Rowan Williams, *Open to Judgement: Sermons and Addresses* (London: Darton, Longman and Todd, 1994), p. 237.
24 Williams, *Open to Judgement*, p. 238.
25 Mary Grey, *Redeeming the Dream: Feminism, Redemption and the Christian Tradition* (London: SPCK, 1989), p. 9.
26 Karl Rahner SJ, *Theological Investigations*, vol. 3: *Theology of the Spiritual Life* (London: Darton, Longman and Todd, 1967), p. 98.
27 Rahner, *Theological Investigations*, vol. 3, p. 100.
28 David Matzko, 'Hazarding theology: theological descriptions and particular lives' (PhD dissertation: Duke University, 1992), p. 4.
29 *Lumen Gentium: Dogmatic Constitution on the Church*, 50–51 in Austin Flannery OP, *Vatican Council II: The Conciliar and Post Conciliar Documents* (Leominster: Fowler Wright, 1981), pp. 411–12.
30 Carter Heyward, *Speaking of Christ: A Lesbian Feminist Voice* (New York: The Pilgrim Press, 1989), p. 62.
31 Heyward, *Speaking of Christ*, pp. 26–7.
32 Heyward, *Speaking of Christ*, p. 28.
33 Heyward, *Speaking of Christ*, p. 28.
34 Carol Gilligan, *In A Different Voice: Psychological Theory and Women's Development* (Cambridge, MA: Harvard University Press, 1982).

35 Rita Nakashima Brock, *Journeys by Heart: A Christology of Erotic Power* (New York: Crossroad, 1988), p. 66.
36 Brock, *Journeys by Heart*, p. 52.
37 Carter Heyward, *Our Passion for Justice: Images of Power, Sexuality and Liberation* (New York: The Pilgrim Press, 1984), p. 97.
38 Heyward, *Our Passion for Justice*, pp. 97–8.
39 Carter Heyward, *Staying Power: Reflections on Gender, Justice and Compassion* (Cleveland: The Pilgrim Press, 1995), pp. 121–33.
40 Avery Dulles, *The Catholicity of the Church* (Oxford: Oxford University Press, 1985), p. 84.
41 Dietrich Bonhoeffer, *The Communion of Saints* (New York: Harper and Row, 1964), pp. 129–30.
42 Heyward, *Speaking of Christ*, pp. 28–9.
43 Heyward, *Speaking of Christ*, p. 29.
44 Grace M. Jantzen, 'Feminism and flourishing: gender and metaphor in feminist theology', *Feminist Theology*, vol. 10 (September 1995), p. 83.
45 Jantzen, 'Feminism and flourishing', p. 2.
46 Jantzen, 'Feminism and flourishing', p. 94.
47 Matthew Fox, *Hildegard of Bingen's Book of Divine Works with Letters and Songs* (Santa Fe: Bear and Co., 1987), p. 379.
48 Rosemary Radford Ruether, 'Ecofeminism and healing ourselves, healing the earth', *Feminist Theology*, vol. 9 (May 1995), p. 61.
49 Ruether, 'Ecofeminism and healing ourselves, healing the earth', p. 61.
50 Ruether, 'Ecofeminism and healing ourselves, healing the earth', p. 61.
51 Sallie McFague, *Models of God: Theology for an Ecological, Nuclear Age* (London: SCM, 1987), p. 72.
52 Peter Brown, *The Cult of the Saints: Its Rise and Function in Latin Christianity* (London: SCM, 1981), p. 87.
53 Brock, *Journeys by Heart*, p. 100.
54 Brock, *Journeys by Heart*, p. 100.
55 Brock, *Journeys by Heart*, p. 101.
56 See, for example, Elaine Graham, 'From space to woman-space', *Feminist Theology*, vol. 9 (May 1995), pp. 11–34.
57 Brock, *Journeys by Heart*, pp. 105–6.

5

Conclusions

In drawing this exploration into a possible feminist theology of sainthood to a close I would like to suggest a number of ways in which the energy of women's saints down the centuries might be befriended and used to inspire, affirm, encourage and challenge those of us engaged in the Christian feminist project today. It is, like the whole of this book, but a preliminary sketch, a broad outline of a map of a largely uncharted territory for feminist Christians. I hope that others will take up my map and step into the land of our history and chart a more precise survey.

Alternative authority

Of all the stories I have read about female saints my favourite concerns a saint little known, particularly in the West, St Elizabeth the Thaumatourgos or Miracle-Worker. She lived in the fifth century in Heraklea with devout Christian parents. By the time she was three she could recite the lives of the saints. Her parents died while she was still young. Elizabeth redistributed their wealth among the poor and went to Constantinople where she entered the convent of St George the Great which was in the charge of an aunt. Elizabeth was eventually to succeed her aunt as abbess.[1] Agnes Dunbar in her short entry on this saint records that Elizabeth

> had in a wonderful degree, the gift of ministering to all the woes and wants of her fellow creatures. She cured diseases, cast out devils, and destroyed an enormous serpent. She fasted forty days, and for many years did not taste bread or oil; went barefooted, and wore a single garment summer and winter; endured extreme cold, but was inflamed with the love of God. For three years she kept her mind's eye fixed on God, but never raised her bodily eye to heaven. During her whole life she never took a bath.[2]

Dunbar, however, skates over what must be the most interesting episode in Elizabeth's career, her destruction of the 'enormous serpent', usually represented as a dragon in Eastern literature. For Elizabeth was a female equivalent of St George with a few interesting differences. To appreciate Elizabeth's story it may help to recall that of George. According to *The Golden Legend*, through which the story became popular in the West, George was a tribune from Cappadocia who, travelling to Silena in Lybia, found the population terrified by a 'plague-bearing dragon' who lived in a pond near the town. To keep the dragon away from the city the townspeople used to feed it two sheep a day, but soon the supply of sheep began to run short and so the people decided to offer one sheep and one man or woman drawn by lot from amongst the townspeople. Eventually the lot fell on the daughter of the king and despite his efforts the townspeople could not be persuaded to spare her life. It was this tearful maiden that George came across when passing by the town.

> George, mounting his horse and arming himself with the sign of the cross, set bravely upon the approaching dragon and, commending himself to God, brandishing his lance, dealt the beast a grievous wound, and forced him to the ground. Then he called to the maiden: 'Have no fear, child! Throw your girdle around the dragon's neck! Don't hesitate!' When she had done this, the dragon rose and followed her like a little dog on a leash.[3]

Some versions of the story have George kill the dragon immediately, but in the version preferred by *The Golden Legend* the dragon was led into the city where George promised the terrified townspeople that if they were baptized he would slay the dragon. They naturally complied and the dragon was killed. George was killed later in the persecution of Diocletian.

The story of Elizabeth is much simpler and less detailed and at one level less dramatic. Elizabeth was given a convent by the Emperor Leo I, but the convent was uninhabitable because a dragon had taken up residence there. Elizabeth, undeterred and armed only with a crucifix, summoned the dragon out of the building, whereupon she simply spat on it and trampled it under her feet.[4] I think that George and Elizabeth can be seen as representing the two models of authority, the patriarchal and the non-patriarchal. George is a soldier, he wears armour and carries a sword. He is protected by a system that gives him the power to perform his duties. He uses this power to protect another patriarchal system, the monarchy of Silena, from a danger that lurks outside its perimeters, threatening the established order. He was not passing when non-royal women or men were awaiting their fate. He is the classic hero. Having tamed the dragon he then engages in manipulative behaviour to enforce the power of yet another patriarchal institution, the Church, for which George later heroically gives his life, having moved on from Silena as a hero. His image is assured both literally, in terms of iconography, and metaphorically. I have not come across any iconographical representations of St Elizabeth the Miracle-Worker (although what a splendid icon her encounter with the dragon would make) and her memory has not been preserved nearly as well as St George's. The emperor, a representative of Christianized patriarchy, gives her a convent for herself and her community of women, but it is tainted by what is *inside* it: something has to be expelled from its walls before this space can become a place of community for them – as a metaphor for the Church it is powerful. Elizabeth does not refuse the gift, nor do she and her friends move in with the dragon and endure the inevitable destructive discomfort, nor do they move in convinced that it will be possible to civilize the beast in the end. She has to deal with the beast head on. Most impressive of all, and perhaps the greatest contrast, is her lack of protective armour or weaponry. Elizabeth does not have the might of a super-power or powers behind her. Her only authority comes from her personal sense of self, inspired and augmented by being connected to others, in other words, her experience of God represented by the crucifix. It is with her own self – her voice, spit and feet – that Elizabeth defeats the dragon. Her purpose is not to bolster authority structures, or to hold a community to ransom, but simply to find safe space for her community. She does not ride off into the sunset but walks into her home.

An amusing poem by U. A. Fanthorpe may serve to highlight the difference between George and Elizabeth. In the poem 'Not my best side', inspired by Uccello's painting of George and the Dragon, each of the three protagonists in the story reflects upon their experience and portrayal. The dragon complains that the artist has not captured his best side. The virgin muses on the fact that she was more attracted to the dragon than to George because she could not determine what he was like 'underneath the hardware'. Finally George speaks, boasting of his qualifications in 'dragon management' and 'virgin reclamation' and his state-of-the-art armour. He cannot understand what the dragon and virgin are complaining about. Surely they want to play their roles, otherwise the 'spear-and-horse-building industries' would collapse. But he finishes:

> What, in any case does it matter what
> You want? You're in my way.[5]

Fanthorpe represents George as the embodiment of patriarchy; the story of Elizabeth is a perfect foil to it. One Eastern theologian referred to her as 'our God-bearing Mother' and it is easy to understand how Christian feminists could see in Elizabeth the bearer of the passionate power of God which through the matrix of right-relationship binds people into communities of defiance, resistance and creativity. Elizabeth, like so many Christian women, was offered bread which turned out to be a stone. But she chose to stand her ground on the boundary, not giving up but not compromising her own vision and needs. These ultimately summoned the dragon out and led to its downfall. Resistance, defiance and creativity (also represented in the memory of her fasting, and approach to clothes and baths!) win the day and Elizabeth lives to enjoy the space she fought for with her friends. There is no 'heroic' ending. It is no doubt a happy accident that Elizabeth's feast day is 24 April, the day after St George's, so that these two saints are officially juxtaposed in the mind of the Church, one representing patriarchal authority and power, the other representing the exact opposite.

This exercise of what we might call 'women's power' is manifested by many of the female saints. This is clearly illustrated among the Christian women of the East who resisted the iconoclastic movement in the Greek Church in the eighth and ninth centuries. The iconoclasm of Leo III and his successors threatened to undermine the humanity of Christ and Mary and the saints. Interestingly, it was women who united to defeat this dehumanizing of the divine and the holy. The Empress Theodora is usually given at least grudging credit for defeating the iconoclasts in 843, building on the previous work of the Empress Irene (for which they were both canonized), but in reality she was aided by women of all classes.[6] Among these was Theodosia, who when her mother died was reported to have purchased three icons and given the rest of her money away. The icons were of Christ, the Virgin Mary and St Anastasia, a fourth-century saint extremely popular in the Greek Church, who all her life co-operated with other women, first her mother, then her maid, and then the spirit of her friend St Theodora, to follow her Christian calling against the intervention and obstruction of men. She was eventually martyred. Theodosia, empowered by the friendship of her saints, and along with the other women who resisted iconoclasm, was part of a riot of mainly female resistance when an image of Christ was removed from over the Aenea Gate in Constantinople in 729. The women knocked over the ladder upon which a soldier was climbing to remove the image. He died in the fall and the women were immediately executed. Theodosia was regarded as the ring-leader and was therefore singled out for a particularly cruel death.[7] Whatever one might think of the tactics used (and there can be no shrinking from the fact that a man was killed), the memory of women acting together to resist with their own bodies a theological error (which would undoubtedly have had a negative effect upon women because women were associated with the bodily, and the iconoclasts wanted to deny that divinity had any connection with the body) is an impressive and inspiring one. Theodosia's memory was preserved in the works of the ninth-century hymnologist Kassione the Nun.[8] Kassione was also involved in the anti-iconoclast movement, for which she suffered persecution. Her hymns are steeped in incarna-tional theology and full of her own experience. Her hymns are about holy women, including 'the woman who has fallen into many sins' of Luke 7. One of her hymns has a series of statements all beginning with the words 'I hate', including 'I hate silence when it is time to speak'.[9] She evidently felt that Theodosia had spoken bravely in a time when it was inappropriate to keep silence and she kept her memory alive through her work. Thus in the iconoclasm crisis we see another example of women standing their ground as women, calling forth their own authority against the super-powers of their day, Church and State in alliance, some having to pay dearly for doing so. Perhaps the nearest thing we have witnessed in our own day is the action of the women of Greenham Common. They stood their ground, only as women, on the boundary of a nuclear airforce base, reviled, hated and feared by many; their authority was undeniable, un-ignorable and ultimately undefeatable because it was so very different from the power it was resisting. In the female saints we have a number of exciting, amusing and affirming examples of women's power in action: power which we might encapsulate in the phrase 'spitting at dragons'.

Authority that extends beyond boundaries

It is undeniably true that some female Christian saints carry with them a history that extends back to before Christianity. A clear example of this is St Brigit of Kildare. More churches were dedicated to her than to St Patrick in Ireland, and her popularity did not wane even when Marianism began to grip Ireland from the twelfth century onwards. Perhaps some of that popularity can be attributed to the fact that Brigit the saint was a memory of the goddess Brigit, represented as the mother goddess in pre-Christian Celtic Ireland, often in triple form. Condren believes that Brigit became the unifying goddess of ancient Ireland, recognized by all tribes and not confined to one piece of territory as other deities were.[10] There are certainly some striking parallels between the two figures. They were both hailed as patrons of poetry, healing and fire. They share certain symbols – serpent, milk, sun, moon, a sacred cow – all symbols of fertility and regeneration. St Brigit's feast day, 1 February, was the major feast of Imbolc in the Celtic calendar, associated with fertility and new life, when Brigit was believed to 'breathe life into the mouth of the dead winter'.[11] According to her *Lives* Brigit was born to her father's slave and was subsequently fostered by a Druid who brought her up and eventually converted to Christianity himself. The chief symbol associated with the saint was the sacred oak from which Kildare ('Church of the Oak') was named. Oaks were, of course, sacred trees in pre-Christian Celtic cultures. At her monastery in Kildare, Brigit and those who came after her kept a sacred fire burning until the thirteenth century when popular outrage at its extinguishing on the orders of the papal legate led to its relighting. The religious community at Kildare was disbanded in the sixteenth century. According to Gerald of Wales, the fire was tended by a member of the community each day for twenty days, and then Brigit was asked to tend it herself. Men were not permitted to go near it. Archaeological evidence suggests that a fire existed nearby in the Iron Age, perhaps indicating that the site at Kildare had been a pre-Christian sacred site. Certainly the whole area around Kildare was known in pre-Christian times as the City of Brigit.[12] Condren believes that the evidence might point towards a college of vestal virgins and thinks that St Brigit took over the symbolic function of vestal virgins, representing the unity, the unbrokenness of Irish culture.

The concerted efforts of hagiographers to represent St Brigit as a pure Christian virgin compliant to Rome and its male representatives have ultimately failed. Stories of her ordination, her non-adoption of the Roman Ordo, her frequent clashes with bishops, make it clear that we are dealing with something subversive and ultimately uncontrollable by Christian orthodoxy. There are several stories of clashes with St Brendan and St Patrick. Condren comments: 'That these saints were contemporaries of each other, or that they even met, is extremely unlikely; the stories reflect struggles between the followers of their various traditions but are valuable accounts of the sexual dynamics at that time.'[13] Her refusal to confess to Brendan, his surprise that neither his name nor that of Patrick's could subdue a sea monster but that her name could, and her tussles with Patrick that eventually led them to divide Ireland between them, all imply Brigit's superiority and stubborn refusal to concede anything to these men. In the stories of St Brigit and other female saints such as St Barbara (whom many believe to be the Christianization of a Graeco-Roman goddess of war), we are put in touch with energies that extend back beyond the dawn of Christianity, energy that then rises again in Christian forms. We are back again to the concept of Sophia, of energy for flourishing that is incarnated in communities and embodied in individuals, that has always existed and played its part in bringing to birth the fluid configuration of beliefs and practices we now identify as Christianity.

The body of Sophia is older than Christianity and is also broader than Christianity although she only carries significant meaning within Christianity. It is important for Christian women to be reminded of this fact for their own spiritual health and survival. But we must not fall into the nostalgia trap of assuming that pre-Christian societies were a golden age for women – they evidently were not – and there is also a question about whether saints like Brigit should be valued, as they are in some feminist circles, just because they give us some connection with 'the goddess'. This is an issue raised by Els Maeckelberghe in her study on feminist interpretations of the Virgin Mary. Maeckelberghe traces Mary Daly's shifting approach to the Virgin. Daly has arrived at an understanding of Mary as an Archimage, a remnant of the goddess moulded by patriarchy into an image reflecting its own dastardly concerns. Yet Mary will not be as pliable as they would wish: by reversing the doctrines super-imposed by Christianity, Daly believes that it is possible to reconnect with the 'power of the parthenogenetic Goddess'. Maeckelberghe asks whether it is possible to disconnect Mary from her Christian roots, whether it is desirable to ignore the 'historical Mary'.[14] She believes the answer is negative, for she wants to identify Mary as a symbol and, as Ricoeur noted, symbols are part of a story and it is only as such that they are symbols. Mary belongs to the Christian story, and 'we cannot isolate Mary and try to fill her up with new meanings apart from the story that she arises from. The possibilities of the Mary symbol are streamlined and limited by the tradition in which she participates.'[15] The same is also true of women saints. To remove them from their Christian historical context is to do violence to their stories and to render them meaningless. They simply become vessels for our own fantasies and agendas, objects for our own manipulation, just they have previously been objects of male manipulation. Yet the stories of Mary and the saints some-times have their origins in a pre-Christian context, just as the story of Jesus and the community that nurtured and surrounded him had its roots in Judaism. Sophia is not confined by the boundaries placed around 'religion' by men; like Brigit, both the goddess and the saint, she casts her cloak to mark her sacred territory, yet its edges cannot be seen, for it has spread wider than our imaginations are pre-pared to grasp. Its energy bubbles up in unlikely places and through unlikely roots but it is energy to be grasped, absorbed and celebrated nevertheless.

Different strategies, same goal

There is no one type of female saint. However much the Church may have tried to mould models of female piety, it has never quite succeeded. Married women, virgins, widows, queens and maids, abbesses and independent women like Joan stand side by side in the saintly canon. Children, adolescents, mature and elderly women sit together in the saintly circle, the illiterate and the scholarly, the domestic and the wild, are all represented. What the Church's official canon lacks in terms of variety is race and Christian affiliation. This partial variety suggests that the route to 'holiness' or in more feminist terms, flourishing, is not narrow even in the tradition's own terms. There is a recognition of a common project amongst a variety of life-styles and choices. Both Christianity and feminism have sometimes fallen into the trap of prescribing and proscribing or ranking certain ways of life for women. The lives of the women saints into which we have dipped demonstrate that a woman in any circumstance is capable of flourishing – as Maya Angelou put it, of thriving with 'passion, compassion, humour and style' – as long as her sense of self is great enough and she is held in a web of affirming relationships, in other words, has an experience of 'beloved community'. This is not to say that women are inevitably confined to certain circumstances or that they should not try and break out of those which they may find destructive to themselves and others. There is an enormous amount of variety in the lives of women saints, variety that should both speak to and challenge modern Christian feminism.

It is this recognition of sameness in difference that allowed people, and sometimes the saints themselves, to experience some kind of important connection with those very different to themselves. A good example of this is the Welsh saint Dwynwen who became the patron of love (a Welsh version of St Valentine but with a great deal more claim to be such a patron). She was a virgin bent on a religious life who implored God to rid her of her love for a man who wanted to enter into a relationship with her. According to her legend, God responded by giving her a potion that cured her of her love but also turned her suitor into a lump of ice. She was then granted three requests. The saint asked for her lover to be defrosted, her ardour for marriage to be completely and indefinitely quenched, and, interestingly, that she might become a supplicant for true lovers, able to grant them either a life together or a cure for their love. So the virgin saint became a source of power for lovers and her shrines at Llanddwyn and in Glamorgan became places of pilgrimage for those whose life she never wanted, but whom she felt for. In Glamorgan her 'bow of destiny', an arch within a cave, became a place of divination. People would toss stones over the arch to determine either the number of years they had to wait before they were to be wed or the number of years they had to endure before they would be able to marry again![16]

In a similar vein St Wilgefortis, or Uncumber, resisted her pagan father's attempts to marry her to a fellow king and prayed that God would disfigure her so that no one would want to marry her. She was answered by the sudden growth of a thick beard. Her father had her crucified. Debate rages between scholars as to whether representations of her in art are in fact representations of Christ. In any case Uncumber became the patron not only of women seeking to resist marriage but also of women who are unhappily married. Unhappy women would leave sacks of oats at her shrines and Dunbar records that English wives had a particular devotion to her. Evidently the saint's ability to help women 'uncumber' themselves from men endeared her to many women, unmarried and married.

A final interesting example is provided in Dorothy Day's relationship with Thérèse of Lisieux. Day found in this unlikely friend, whose life was so very different from her own, an energy that both inspired and challenged her. She particularly valued the saint's determination to live in the world of reality, to see things as they really were and her determination to live a life of mercy.[17] But it is Thérèse's ordinariness that appealed to Day most, and her conviction that the ordinary things of the world can become transformative. Day saw in her own movement the army of 'little saints' that Thérèse had promised to send after her death. Matzko believes that 'insofar as Day had a political vision, Thérèse is one of the representations of this vision'.[18] It is hard to grasp that a woman as radical and unconventional as Day could have been influenced by the 'Little Flower' but it is clear that she was. This transfer of energy from one very different life to another which went on between women of past ages is still available to those who wish to partake of it today.

The different lives also reveal different strategies for survival, flourishing, and creating 'beloved community' amongst women. It is easy to concentrate on those women who, like Catherine of Siena or Teresa of Avila or the Beguines, sought to find a way of living outside of pre-existing church structures, but there were many women who went to great lengths to get into the heart of the ecclesiastical establishment. Mention has already been made of the phenomenon of transvestite saints who dressed as men and often lived all their lives in a male persona in order to enter a religious order or to assume the life of a recluse. St Hildegund, a twelfth-century German saint, is an interesting example of this phenomenon. Hildegund first assumed a male disguise and the name Joseph at her father's suggestion, when accompanying him on a pilgrimage to Jerusalem. He died during the voyage, but she retained the identity and from this point in the story all her biographers refer to her as Joseph and assume she was a man. Hildegund thereafter embarked on various travels during which she was frequently the victim of criminals and lack of justice. Eventually she went and lived with a recluse named Matilda 'who made no scruple of receiving him, either because he had confided his secret to her, or because she considered herself above suspicion or scandal'.[19] There Hildegund studied diligently until gossip about the relationship between the two led her, after much anguished reflection, to enter a monastic community in Schönau. Although she was so indiscreet as to almost invite detection, this did not happen until after her death when, as Agnes Dunbar puts it, 'they discovered that he wore stays'.[20]

Hildegund's male disguise enabled her to move about freely in the world and to pursue a vocation. It is possible to interpret such behaviour as ultimately counterproductive for the feminist project, for by disguising themselves in this way the women implicitly acknowledge and accept that the sacred is male space. But there may be another way of interpreting this kind of activity. What these women did was to walk through the walls of patriarchy, in disguise, under cover, using all their ingenuity and cunning, rather like some of the ancient representations of the atonement: God disguising himself in human form tricks the devil into swallowing him up in death as a bait tricks a fish; only too late does Satan realize that what he has swallowed he cannot contain or digest, and he chokes to death. The female saints in male disguise penetrated to the heart of male space and then demonstrated that it was not male space any more. Their disguise may only have been revealed after death but, even so, the revelation of the real identities of Brother Joseph and the others served notice that women cannot be contained within the confines that the church fathers had built for them. In penetrating to the heart of a patriarchal system these women not so much blazed a trail for others to follow but laid the charges which would and will eventually contribute to its destruction. Male space, when it also becomes true female space, is changed beyond measure. For that change to happen, some women have to venture into it, either in disguise or upon male sufferance. It is one important aspect of the common project of building up 'beloved community'. In the story of Hildegund we see Brother Joseph co-operating with Matilda, a woman who had chosen to be on the boundary. They have a common purpose. Boundary dwellers and 'insiders' are engaged in the same enterprise. This is a lesson the Christian feminist movement needs constantly to relearn, as anger, hurt and tension caused by some choosing to dwell on boundaries and some to live at the heart of the system (perhaps, for example, as priests) often divides us.

Mutual questioning

Christian feminists read the lives of the saints through the spectacles of suspicion. There is much in the lives of the female saints that we find deeply unpalatable: ambiguous attitudes to the body and self; philosophical and theological dualism; uncritical acceptance of male authority; behaviour we find might difficult to endorse (such as Theodosia's attack on the soldier). We cannot simply accept and presuppose the 'holiness' of a sainted woman's complete life. We might recognize, celebrate and tap into her energy as manifested in particular actions or ways of being, whilst also acknowledging that not all of her life was about flourishing, that some of it may have been about withering of herself and others. We can acknowledge this because we recognize it in ourselves. We are aware of how difficult it is to flourish when brought up and caught in a network of structures that are not conducive to flourishing, that teach us to be disconnected from others and concerned only with ourselves, and that work upon the principles of violent competition. We are aware of the extent to which this system is written upon our hearts, and how much easier in the short term it is to fall into its pattern of relating. Flourishing in such an environment requires gargantuan amounts of effort and most of us do not have the energy to sustain it constantly. We are lucky if we are able to manifest it in one part of our lives. It is part of the dynamics of friendship as represented in feminist discourse that mutual questioning and criticism are not antithetical to friendship but an important part of the building up of mutuality. So our friendships with the saints, if they are to be meaningful and nourishing, must include a critical dimension.

But by the same token we must allow ourselves to be open to the judgement of the saints, for they ask some uncomfortable questions of us. Most importantly they demand that we who recognize them indulgently as women of their time, living under the constraints of a particular history, recognize ourselves, our ideas, our visions and our practices as similarly historically conditioned. They kindly warn us against associating our lives with divine truth. Yet they also invite us to trust our own experience as women. I have chosen not to focus on the theology of the theologian saints like Teresa of Avila, but a dip into the theological writings of the female saints demonstrates how deeply they drew on their experience as women and how different, therefore, their theology was from that of the male establishment.

To give but one brief example: St Brigid of Sweden, a rather neglected theologian in feminist study, perhaps because of her emphasis on suffering and death, had a deeply embodied theology. Her visions were experienced in and through her body and she had a non-dualistic understanding of the relationship between body and soul. She preached that God was everywhere and 'ungraspable'; nothing was profane, all was sacred. Animals, humans and non-animate beings she saw as intimately related and equally open to God's presence, and all of them sacraments of his presence. Her theology is also one of process: nothing is fixed or ordained; every-thing is in the process of becoming. Only the refusal to love can reduce a person to nothingness. Even her emphasis upon sacrificial suffering is grounded in relationship and her personal experience of motherhood, as Brigitta Trotzig explains:

The risen one bears his wounds for all eternity as a sign that the inner-most point in people, their holy of holies, is a place of sacrifice – whether it happens to occur on a cross or on a bed of love or in 'the dark shed' in which a mother gives birth . . . There is no contradiction in the fact that Birgitta's experience of the suffering saviour, he who expends himself, sacrifices himself, grew out of and was deepened by her experience of herself as one who, tangibly and biologically, was primarily created to give birth, to give herself, to sacrifice herself.[21]

Contemporary feminists might wince at this interpretation of mother-hood but can still appreciate the radical nature of Brigid's theology within her context. The message is to be creative with what you have, but not to fall into the trap of thinking that what you have is pure divinity. The saints also challenge us with their life-changing and often life-risking action for the sake of their faith. We who are Christian feminists talk constantly of transforming the world. Our saintly friends remind us that this must begin with our own lives. We must put our bodies where our ideals are. And there are plenty of examples of women, like Elizabeth of Hungary, who had to balance responsibilities and commitments with a radical calling, as most of us have to do and which we often use as an excuse for doing very little. They challenge us to weave a faith worth offering our lives for, a belief-system worthy of passion. They demand that we ensure that our lives will inspire, encourage and nourish the women who come after us, that we help them to flourish by flourishing ourselves, that we keep the dangerous memory alive.

Eco-friendship

Reconnection to the earth and all life upon it has been part of the feminist project for a long time; alienation from and consequent exploitation of the non-human world has arisen from the dualism that is the heart of patriarchal darkness. The lives of the saints present us with stories of men and women who lived their lives against the grain of this alienation and exploitation, who recognized the sacred in the life around them where others simply saw 'its', objects for exploita-tion. There are certainly stories which, from an ecofeminist perspective, are not particularly palatable, for example, of grateful anthropo morphic animals becoming 'servants' to saints who have rescued them; but there are stories in which animals and saints are brought into the circle dance of friendship, which acknowledges and celebrates difference but which also recognizes and celebrates commonality.

Helen Waddell included only one woman in her study of 'beasts and saints'. The saint in question was Werburga of Chester, an abbess whose farm was plagued by a flock of wild geese. Werburga ordered her steward to summon the geese into a barn and they duly obeyed. One of the farm hands, however, took one of the geese and ate it. The next day the saint visited the geese and told them to stop plundering her corn and then let them go. But the birds refused to fly away and eventually managed to communicate their displeasure that one of their number had been consumed. Werburga gathered up the departed goose's bones and resurrected it. The story goes that since then no wild geese have fed upon the crops of that farm.[22] This story can be read either as a celebration of the saint's power, or as a story extolling co-operation between different creatures and non-exploitation. In Celtic Christianity the wild goose was a symbol of the Holy Spirit and wild geese like humans flourish when they are in the company of their fellows. Werburga recognized in them a dignity that should not be violated.

One of the best known of the Welsh saints is St Melangell, who fled to Wales from Ireland in the seventh century to avoid marriage. There she lived as a hermit until discovered by the prince of Powys sheltering a hare which he had been hunting. His dogs would not approach the woman and the hunting horn stuck to the lips of its player. The prince asked her to go with him, but when she refused he gave her some land with rights of sanctuary, so no one was ever again to kill hares there. Hares recognized her as a friend and flocked to her. Hares became known as *wyn Melangell* (Melangell's lambs) and people would call after a hare *Duw a Melangell a'th gadwo* (God and Saint Melangell preserve you) in the hope that it would escape human hunters.[23] The friendship between saints and the world around them (which extended beyond animals to the earth), most prominent in the Celtic tradition, provides example, inspiration and energy to draw upon in constructing theologies and strategies for ecological survival. There is within the lives of the saints a dangerous memory of resistance to the 'stewardship' mentality that has dominated Christianity and has been theologized as a licence to exploit. Our ancestors in faith, at least in some pockets of the world, recognized that friendship with God involves friendship with the non-human world, and those particularly close to God manifest particular closeness to nature.

Solidarity in struggle against the Church

For a large proportion of women saints the Church was part of the problem rather than the solution. The experience of Catherine of Siena of the Church descending upon her shoulders is one that could be echoed by thousands of saintly women, for the male hierarchy of the Church invariably tried to prevent these women from flourishing and sought to channel them into patterns of lives that would tame their spirits. Whilst male saints wrestled with the devil, women wrestled with men. Gilbert Márkus points out that the tradition of the saints reminds those of us who today struggle for justice with the weight of the Church bearing down upon our shoulders, threatening to crush our spirit and drain our energy, that it is we who are the bearers of the mainstream of the Christianity, not our crushers. The saints give us the hermeneutical key to understand and correct the reversing that goes on in patriarchy: what are claimed today as 'orthodoxy' and 'heresy' are often the exact opposite in terms of Christian history.

I hope that I have shown that it is possible, to use Daly's imagery, to take the hags out of hagiography and construct a feminist theology of sainthood that does no injustice either to the women concerned or to the principles of feminist theology. I hope I have made some kind of sense of the desire of a sizeable number of Christian women in all ages and circumstances to feel the friendship of women who have gone before and perhaps encouraged women for whom sainthood is not part of their tradition to tap into the embodied energy of our ancestors in faith. Their example, energy and encouragement offers us some of the friendship which enables us to flourish. We might recall Heyward's words quoted in Chapter 1:

> Heroes show us who we are *not*. Helpers show us who we *are*. As individual supermen/wonderwomen, heroes diminish our senses of relational, or shared, power. Helpers call us forth into our power in relation and strengthen our senses of ourselves.

I have tried to demonstrate that the women saints can be helpers and are not heroes. May we be worthy of their legacy, so that one day those who are today the daughters of our generation or their grand-daughters will be able to gain strength from us and call us to be present in their struggle to flourish. Simone Weil once declared that 'the world today needs saints, new saints, saints of genius'.[24] We have to call forth spiritual power in each other and allow the women who have gone before us to do the same, because we are the saints Weil longed for.

NOTES

1 Eva Topping, *Holy Mothers of Orthodoxy* (Minneapolis: Light and Life, 1987), pp. 71–2.

2 Agnes B. C. Dunbar, *A Dictionary of Saintly Women*, vol. 1 (London: George Bell and Sons, 1904), p. 257.

3 Jacobus de Voragine, *The Golden Legend: Readings on the Saints*, translated by William Granger Ryan (Princeton: Princeton University Press, 1993) vol. 1, p. 239.

4 Topping, *Holy Mothers of Orthodoxy*, pp. 71–2.

5 U. A. Fanthorpe, 'Not my best side' in Linda France, *Sixty Women Poets* (Newcastle upon Tyne: Bloodaxe Books, 1993), p. 128.

6 Topping, *Holy Mothers of Orthodoxy*, p. 14.

7 Topping, *Holy Mothers of Orthodoxy*, p. 14; and Dunbar, *Dictionary of Saintly Women*, vol. 2, p. 257.

8 Topping, *Holy Mothers of Orthodoxy*, p. 12.

9 Topping, *Holy Mothers of Orthodoxy*, p. 32.

10 Mary Condren, *The Serpent and the Goddess: Women, Religion and Power in Celtic Ireland* (San Francisco: HarperSanFrancisco, 1989), p. 60.

11 Condren, *The Serpent and the Goddess*, p. 58.

12 Condren, *The Serpent and the Goddess*, pp. 66–7.

13 Condren, *The Serpent and the Goddess*, p. 75.

14 Els Maeckelberghe, *Desperately Seeking Mary: A Feminist Appropriation of a Traditional Religious Symbol* (Kampen: KOK Pharos, 1994), pp. 25–9.

15 Maeckelberghe, *Desperately Seeking Mary*, p. 149.

16 Elissa R. Henken, *Traditions of the Welsh Saints* (Cambridge: D. S. Brewer, 1987), pp. 228–31.

17 David Matthew Matzko, 'Postmodernism, saints and scoundrels', *Modern Theology*, vol. 9 (January 1993), p. 32.

18 Matzko, 'Postmodernism, saints and scoundrels', p. 32.

19 Dunbar, *A Dictionary of Saintly Women*, vol. 1, p. 390.

20 Dunbar, *A Dictionary of Saintly Women*, vol. 1, p. 390.

21 Brigitta Trotzig, 'The Crucified, he whom I saw: Brigid of Sweden', *Cross Currents* (Summer/Fall 1985), pp. 297–8.

22 Helen Waddell, *Beasts and Saints*, introduced and edited by Esther de Waal (London: Darton, Longman and Todd, 1995), pp. 63–6.

23 Henken, *Traditions of the Welsh Saints*, p. 217.

24 Cited in John A. Coleman SJ, 'Conclusion: after sainthood' in John Stratton Hawley (ed.), *Saints and Virtues* (Berkeley: University of California Press, 1987), p. 223.

Bibliography

Carol J. Adams, 'Naming, denial and sexual violence', *Miriam's Song*, vol. 5 (n.d.).

Prudence Allen, 'Hildegard of Bingen's philosophy of sex identity', *Thought*, vol. 64 (September 1989).

Clarissa Atkinson, *Mystic and Pilgrim: The Book and World of Margery Kempe* (Ithaca: Cornell University Press, 1981).

Clarissa Atkinson, Constance H. Buchanan and Margaret R. Miles, *Immaculate and Powerful: The Female in Sacred Image and Social Reality* (Boston: Beacon Press, 1985).

Ann Ball, *Modern Saints: Their Lives and Faces* (Rockford: Tan Books, 1983).

Bandung Limited, *Hell's Angel: Mother Teresa of Calcutta* (transcript; London: Bandung Limited, 1994).

Bruce A. Beatie, 'Saint Katherine of Alexandria: traditional themes and the development of a medieval German hagiographic narrative', *Speculum: A Journal of Medieval Studies*, vol. 52 (October 1977).

Clyde Binfield (ed.), *Sainthood Revisioned: Studies in Hagiography and Biography* (Sheffield: Sheffield Academic Press, 1995).

Renate Blumenfeld-Kosinski and Timea Szell (eds), *Images of Sainthood in Medieval Europe* (Ithaca: Cornell University Press, 1991).

Dietrich Bonhoeffer, *The Communion of Saints* (New York: Harper and Row, 1964).

Lynne C. Boughton, 'From pious legend to feminist fantasy: distinguishing hagiographical license from apostolic practice in the *Acts of Paul/Acts of Thecla*', *Journal of Religion*, vol. 71 (1991).

Rita Nakashima Brock, *Journeys by Heart: A Christology of Erotic Power* (New York: Crossroad, 1988).

Joanne Carlson Brown and Carole R. Bohn (eds), *Christianity, Patriarchy and Abuse* (Cleveland: The Pilgrim Press, 1989).

Peter Brown, *The Cult of the Saints: Its Rise and Function in Latin Christianity* (London: SCM, 1981).

Caroline Bynum, *Holy Feast and Holy Fast: The Religious Significance of Food to Medieval Women* (Berkeley: University of California Press, 1987).

Marina Chavchavadze (ed.), *Man's Concern with Holiness* (London: Hodder and Stoughton, 1970).

Ronda Chervin, 'Wholeness and holiness in the women saints', *Studies in Formative Spirituality*, vol. 9 (1985).

Gillian Cloke, *This Female Man of God: Women and Spiritual Power in the Patristic Age, AD 350–450* (London: Routledge, 1995).

Mary Collins OSB, 'Daughters of the Church: the four Theresas', *Concilium*, no. 182 (1985).

Mary Condren, *The Serpent and the Goddess: Women, Religion and Power in Celtic Ireland* (San Francisco: HarperSanFrancisco, 1989).

J. W. Conn, 'Thérèse of Lisieux from a feminist perspective', *Spiritual Life*, vol. 28 (Winter 1982).

Barbara Corrado Pope, 'A heroine without heroics: the Little Flower and her times', *Church History*, vol. 57 (March 1988).

Lawrence Cunningham, *The Meaning of Saints* (San Francisco: Harper and Row, 1980).

Lawrence Cunningham, 'A decade of research on the saints: 1980–1990', *Theological Studies*, vol. 53 (Summer 1992).

Mary Daly, *Gyn/Ecology: The Metaethics of Radical Feminism* (London: The Women's Press, 1979).

M. Dorgan, 'St Teresa of Avila: woman and waverer', *Cross Currents*, vol. 32 (1982).

Eamon Duffy, *The Stripping of the Altars: Traditional Religion in England 1400–1580* (New Haven: Yale University Press, 1992).

Avery Dulles, *The Catholicity of the Church* (Oxford: Oxford University Press, 1985).

Agnes B. C. Dunbar, *A Dictionary of Saintly Women* (2 vols; London: George Bell and Sons, 1904).

David Hugh Farmer, *The Oxford Dictionary of Saints* (Oxford: Oxford University Press, 1978).

Elisabeth Schüssler Fiorenza, *In Memory of Her: A Feminist Theological Reconstruction of Christian Origins* (London: SCM, 1983).

Elisabeth Schussler Fiorenza, *Discipleship of Equals: A Critical Feminist Ekklesia-logy of Liberation* (London: SCM, 1993).

Austin Flannery OP, *Vatican Council II: The Conciliar and Post Conciliar Documents* (Leominster: Fowler Wright, 1981).

Matthew Fox, *Hildegard of Bingen's Book of Divine Works with Letters and Songs* (Santa Fe: Bear and Co., 1987).

Katherine and Charles H. George, 'Roman Catholic sainthood and social status: a statistical and analytical study', *Journal of Religion*, vol. 35, no. 2 (April 1955).

Dennis Graviss, 'Ms Teresa of Avila: the experience of the 20th century through 16th century eyes', *Studies in Formative Spirituality*, vol. 5 (1984).

Mary Grey, *Redeeming the Dream: Feminism, Redemption and Christian Tradition* (London: SPCK, 1989).

Mary Grey, *The Wisdom of Fools? Seeking Revelation for Today* (London: SPCK, 1993).

Daphne Hampson, *Theology and Feminism* (Oxford: Basil Blackwell, 1990).

Susan Haskins, *Mary Magdalen: Myth and Metaphor* (London: Harper-Collins, 1993).

John Stratton Hawley (ed.), *Saints and Virtues* (Berkeley: University of California Press, 1987).

Thomas J. Heffernan, *Sacred Biography: Saints and Their Biographers in the Middle Ages* (Oxford: Oxford University Press, 1988).

Elissa R. Henken, *Traditions of the Welsh Saints* (Cambridge: D. S. Brewer, 1987).

Elissa R. Henken, *The Welsh Saints: A Study in Pattern Lives* (Cambridge: D. S. Brewer, 1991).

Carter Heyward, *Our Passion for Justice: Images of Power, Sexuality and Liberation* (New York: The Pilgrim Press, 1984).

Carter Heyward, *Speaking of Christ: A Lesbian Feminist Voice* (New York: The Pilgrim Press, 1989).

Carter Heyward, *Touching Our Strength: The Erotic as Power and the Love of God* (San Francisco: Harper and Row, 1989).

Carter Heyward, *Staying Power: Reflections on Gender, Justice, and Compassion* (Cleveland: The Pilgrim Press, 1995).

Eduardo Hoornaert, *The Memory of the Christian People* (Tunbridge Wells: Burns and Oates, 1988).

Mary E. Hunt, *Fierce Tenderness: A Feminist Theology of Friendship* (New York: Crossroad, 1991).

Linda Hurcombe (ed.), *Sex and God: Some Varieties of Women's Religious Experience* (London: Routledge, 1987).

Catherine Innes-Parker, 'Sexual violence and the female reader: symbolic "rape" in the saints' lives of the Katherine group', *Women's Studies*, vol. 24, no. 3 (1995).

Grace M. Jantzen, 'Feminism and flourishing: gender and metaphor in feminist theology', *Feminist Theology*, vol. 10 (September 1995).

Steven L. Kaplan, 'Religion, subsistence, and social control: the uses of Saint Genevieve', *Eighteenth Century Studies*, vol. 13 (1979).

Sean Kelly and Rosemary Rogers, *Saints Preserve Us!* (London: Robson Books, 1995).

Eric Waldron Kemp, *Canonisation and Authority in the Western Church* (Oxford. Oxford University Press, 1948).

Brother Kenneth CGA, *Saints of the Twentieth Century* (London and Oxford: Mowbray, 1987).

Richard Kieckhefer and George D. Bond, *Sainthood: Its Manifestation in World Religions* (Berkeley: University of California Press, 1988).

Bernhard Lang, 'The sexual lives of the saints: towards an anthropology of Christian heaven', *Journal of Religion and Religions*, vol. 17 (1987).

Mary Luti, '"A marriage well arranged": Teresa of Avila and Fray Jeronimo Gracián de la Madre de Dios', *Studia Mystica*, vol. 12 (Spring 1989).

James Wm McClendon, *Biography As Theology: How Life Stories Can Remake Today's Theology* (New York: Abingdon Press, 1974).

Sallie McFague, *Models of God: Theology for an Ecological, Nuclear Age* (London: SCM, 1987).

Els Maeckelberghe, *Desperately Seeking Mary: A Feminist Appropriation of a Traditional Religious Symbol* (Kampen: KOK Pharos, 1994).

Gilbert Márkus OP, *The Radical Tradition: Saints in the Struggle for Justice and Peace* (London: Darton, Longman and Todd, 1992).

David Matthew Matzko, 'Postmodernism, saints and scoundrels', *Modern Theology*, vol. 9 (January 1993).

John Mecklin, *The Passing of the Saint* (Chicago: University of Chicago Press, 1941).

Johann Baptist Metz, *Faith in History and Society: Toward a Practical Fundamentalist Society* (New York: Seabury Press, 1980).

J. Giles Milhaven, 'A medieval lesson on bodily knowing: women's experience and men's thought', *Journal of the American Academy of Religion*, vol. 57, no. 2 (Summer 1989).

Mary Neill OP and Ronda Chervin, *Great Saints, Great Friends* (New York, Alba House, 1989).

Michael Perham, *The Communion of Saints: An Examination of the Place of the Christian Dead in the Belief, Worship, and Calendars of the Church* (London: Alcuin Club/SPCK, 1980).

Karl Rahner SJ, *Theological Investigations*, vol. 3: *Theology of the Spiritual Life* (London: Darton, Longman and Todd, 1967).

Margaret A. Rees (ed.), *Teresa de Jesús and Her World* (Leeds: Trinity and All Saints' College, 1981).

Rosemary Radford Ruether, 'Ecofeminism and healing ourselves, healing the earth', *Feminist Theology*, vol. 9 (May 1995).

Rosemary Radford Ruether and Eleanor McLaughlin, *Women of Spirit: Female Leadership in the Jewish and Christian Traditions* (New York: Simon and Schuster, 1979).

Victoria Sackville-West, *The Eagle and the Dove: A Study in Contrasts – St Teresa of Avila, St Thérèse of Lisieux* (London: Michael Joseph, 1943).

Karen Scott, 'St Catherine of Siena "Apostola"', *Church History*, vol. 61 (March 1992).

Edward C. Sellner, 'Brigit of Kildare: a study in the liminality of women's spiritual power', *Cross Currents*, vol. 39 (Winter 1989–90).

W. J. Sheils and Diana Wood (eds), *Women in the Church: Papers Read at the 1989 Summer Meeting and the 1990 Winter Meeting of the Ecclesiastical History Society* (Oxford: Basil Blackwell, 1990).

Elizabeth Stuart, *Just Good Friends: Towards a Lesbian and Gay Theology of Relationships* (London: Mowbray, 1995).

C. H. Talbot, *The Life of Christina of Markyate, a Twelfth Century Recluse* (Oxford: Oxford University Press, 1959).

John M. Theilman, 'Political canonisation and political symbolism in medieval England', *Journal of British Studies*, vol. 29 (July 1990).

Thérèse of Lisieux, *The Story of a Soul* (Wheathampstead: Anthony Clarke Books, 1951).

Patrick Thomas, *Candle in the Darkness: Celtic Spirituality from Wales* (Llandysul: Gomer Press, 1993).

Anne Thompson, 'Shaping a saint's Life: Frideswide of Oxford', *Medium Aevum*, vol. 63, no. 1 (1994).

Eva Catafygiotu Topping, *Holy Mothers of Orthodoxy* (Minneapolis: Light and Life, 1987).

Brigitta Trotzig, 'The Crucified, he whom I saw: Brigid of Sweden', *Cross Currents* (Summer/Fall 1985).

Elizabeth Usherwood, *Women First: Biographies of Catholic Women in the Forefront of Change* (London: Sheed and Ward, 1989).

Walter Vandereychen and Ron van Deth, *From Fasting Saints to Anorexic Girls: The History of Self-Starvation* (London: Athlone Press, 1994).

Jacobus de Voragine, *The Golden Legend: Readings on the Saints*, translated by William Granger Ryan (2 vols; Princeton: Princeton University Press, 1993).

Helen Waddell, *Beasts and Saints*, introduced and edited by Esther de Waal (London: Darton, Longman and Todd, 1995).

Michael Walsh (ed.), *Butler's Lives of the Saints* (Tunbridge Wells: Burns and Oates, 1985).

Benedicta Ward, *Signs and Wonders: Saints, Miracles and Prayers from the Fourth Century to the Fourteenth* (Aldershot: Variorum, 1992).

Marina Warner, *Joan of Arc: The Image of Female Heroism* (London: Vintage, 1991).

Alison Webster, *Found Wanting: Women, Christianity and Sexuality* (London: Cassell, 1995).

Donald Weinstein and Rudolph M. Bell, *Saints and Society: The Two Worlds of Western Christendom, 1000–1700* (Chicago: University of Chicago Press, 1982).

Sharon Welch, *Communities of Resistance and Solidarity: A Feminist Theology of Liberation* (Maryknoll, NY: Orbis Books, 1985).

Sharon Welch, *A Feminist Ethic of Risk* (Minneapolis: Fortress Press, 1990).

Johannes Wilber, 'Saints, near-saints and society: religious syncretism in Latin America', *Journal of Latin American Lore*, vol. 14 (Summer 1988).

Stephen Wilson (ed.), *Saints and Their Cults: Studies in Religious Sociology, Folklore and History* (Cambridge: Cambridge University Press, 1983).

B. A. Windeatt, *The Book of Margery Kempe* (Harmondsworth: Penguin, 1985).

Kenneth L. Woodward, *Making Saints: Inside the Vatican: Who Become Saints, Who Do Not and Why* (London: Chatto and Windus, 1991).

Stephen Woodward, 'The provenance of the term "Saints": a *religions-geschichtliche* study', *Journal of the Evangelical Theological Society*, vol. 24 (June 1981).

Edith Wyschogrod, *Saints and Postmodernism: Revisioning Moral Philosophy* (Chicago: University of Chicago Press, 1990).